THE AMERICAN REPUBLIC MANIFESTUM

2012

THE ART OF A REVOLUTION IN AMERICA:

THE RESURRECTION OF THE AMERICAN REPUBLIC

"All things being equal, the simplest explanation is probably the correct one."
- Occam's Razor

"Strange times are those in which we live when old and young are taught in falsehoods school. And the one man that dares to tell the truth is called at once a lunatic and a fool"
– Plato

Written By: *An American*

TABLE OF CONTENTS

The enumeration in the Constitution, of certain rights, shall not be construed to deny or disparage others retained by The People. --The Ninth Amendment

"When we contemplate the fall of empires and the extinction of nations of the Ancient World, we see but little to excite our regrets than the mouldering ruins of pompous palaces, magnificent museums, lofty pyramids and walls and towers of the most costly workmanship; but when the empire of America shall fall, the subject for contemplative sorrow will be infinitely greater than crumbling brass and marble can inspire. It will not then be said, 'Here stood a temple of vast antiquity; here rose a babel of invisible height; or there a palace of sumptuous extravagance; but here, ah, painful thought! the noblest of work of human wisdom, the grandest scene of human glory, the fair cause of Freedom rose and fell."

Thomas Paine

Victory likes careful preparation amat victoria curam

Resolve: America, our Homeland, has lost its way and requires help

from us all. America's government has not lived up to the promise of the

Constitution, Natural Law, the Law of Promise, and the just system of Law

and Trusts... axiom. A People's Republic.

The current American Constitution is a Manifestum of ideas and promises

that guarantee certain inalienable civil liberties to all who live within its

borders. To insure that those rights and privileges are guaranteed to

citizens, there must exist an accord between a well-armed militia defending the Homeland (America), and its people. In return, The People of America must defend and support the Homeland militia at all costs. This symbiotic relationship, is vital for any government of this type to flourish. This vital relationship does not exist in America anymore thus our current demise. The People of America must form and restructure a new Congress that better represents their interests. This would move The People (Public) towards perfecting the current government into one that truly takes care of its people and guarantees with full support the rights and privileges due Americans. People, (i.e., human beings), are the most valued natural resource that any nation can have. Without this resource, all you have is earth.

Liberty and justice for all are but ideas put into words. If we are to have true liberty in America, then we must take back what was stolen from us all: our freedoms, dignity, and respect. We must replace and reinstate the proper representation for Americans: the Government. If this stand is not taken, America will continue down the same road of bad government, which will keep *allowing the wolves to manage the chicken farm.* We as a people, and as a nation, have not lived up to some of the basic American principles written so long ago; *that government of The People, by The People, for The People, shall not perish from the earth.*

There has been no separation of God and government. It is not God who should be expected to save us. On the contrary, The People of America should be in charge of saving themselves. Americans should be trusted to manage their destinies thru honest dialogue and organized labor supported by government. America can rebuild under new laws and orders. This will set a renewed paradigm for the rest of the world to respect and adhere to, for a nation is not measured by wealth, but by deeds.

Every American should read and understand their Declaration of Independence from Brettaniai, because this excerpt is our reason for change not treason or anarchy thru violence.

Excerpt:

"We hold these truths to be self-evident, that all men are created equal, that they are endowed by their Creator with certain inalienable Rights that among these are Life, Liberty and the pursuit of Happiness. — That to secure these rights, Governments are instituted among Men, deriving their just powers from the consent of the governed, — That whenever any Form of Government becomes destructive of these ends, it is the Right of The People to alter or to abolish it, and to institute new Government, laying its foundation on such principles and organizing its powers in such form, as to them shall seem most likely to affect their Safety and Happiness. Prudence, indeed, will dictate that Governments long established should not be changed for light and transient causes; and accordingly all

experience hath shewn that mankind are more disposed to suffer, while evils are sufferable than to right themselves by abolishing the forms to which they are accustomed. But when a long train of abuses and usurpations, pursuing invariably the same Object evinces a design to reduce them under absolute Despotism, it is their right, it is their duty, to throw off such Government, and to provide new Guards for their future security."

Every American should realize that the very words agreed upon in 1776 have long been misinterpreted to satisfy those who were in power then, and today.

The Articles of Confederation and Perpetual Union was written as a precursor to the final draft of the Constitution of America, 1776 - 1787 and finally ratified in 1781 to only be replaced by the current constitution of 1789. Those too, were just words not followed to the letter.

A group of disenchanted men for their own purposes and intents wrote manifestos for new government for America. Most importantly, if the ideas of women were included in the drafting's of these Manifesto's, it was certainly not public knowledge. This was one of the greatest injustices.

Women are a key component in the successes of any nation and its people. Both male and female must share America, so it makes sense that both must collaborate to form a perfect Government.

Religious belief systems should not play any role or influence in American government. World history has evidenced for centuries that religion has been linked to the downfall of many government institutions.

Interestingly, any influence from extraterrestrials has also been kept from the masses, which has been for good reason. If Americans were made privy to this truth, there would be chaos. Those who have been allowed into that universal arena have manipulated influences from these beings. It is not so surprising that extraterrestrials that have visited and made earth their home are still maintaining a purposeful distance from the masses. Having been documented as being present on this planet for centuries, some of them have a well-founded mistrust of us.

This new Manifestum of truths for new government was written by, and for, The People of America in order to form a perfect Republic. This new Congress and new Republic will be created with new rules of law.

This Manifestum does not profess to have all the answers, but will attempt to present fresh new ideas. This Manifestum is intended to incite and instigate all Americans into a state of flux that will ultimately lead to a civil revolution. Revolution will replace everything that is not in the best interest for Americans. A true government of The People, and for The People, will be the intended result. This Manifestum is not just words on paper, but also a declaration of action to inform the misinformed.

What have you done for America, your Homeland?

"We hold these truths to be self-evident, that all men and women are created equal, that they are endowed by their Creator with certain inalienable Rights that among these are Life, Liberty and the pursuit of Happiness."

The Declaration of Independence from the United States of America, Draft

Action of First Continental Congress, December 21, 2012; The Unanimous Declaration of Independence from the United States of America.

WHEN in the Course of human Events, it becomes necessary for one People to dissolve the Political Bands which have connected them with another, and to assume among the Powers of the Earth, the separate and equal Station to which the Laws of Nature and of Nature's God entitle them, a decent Respect to the Opinions of Humans requires that they should declare the causes which impel them to the Separation. WE hold these Truths to be self-evident, that all Men and Women are created equal, that they are endowed by their Creator with certain inalienable Rights, that among these are Life, Liberty, and the Pursuit of Happiness-**That to secure these Rights, Governments are instituted among Men and Women, deriving their just Powers from the Consent of the Governed,** that whenever any Form of Government becomes destructive of these Ends, it is the Right of The People to alter or to abolish it, and to institute new Government, laying its Foundation no such Principles, and organizing its Powers in such Form, as to them shall seem most likely to affect their Safety and Happiness. Prudence, indeed, will dictate that Governments long established should not be changed for light and transient Causes; and accordingly all Experience hath shown, that Humans are more disposed to suffer, while Evils are sufferable, than to right themselves by abolishing the Forms to which they are accustomed. But when a long Train of Abuses and Usurpations, pursuing invariably the same Object, evinces a Design to reduce them under absolute Despotism, it is their Right, it is their Duty, to throw off such Government, and to provide new Guards of their future Security. Such has been the patient Sufferance of these Peoples; and such is now the Necessity, which constrains them to alter their former Systems of Government. The History of the past and present Presidents of the United States of America is a History of repeated Injuries and Usurpations, all having in direct Object, the Establishment of an absolute Tyranny over these States and its people. To prove this, let Facts be submitted to a candid World. He (The Powers That Be) has refused his Assent to Laws, the most wholesome and necessary for the public Good. He has forbidden his Governors to pass

Laws of immediate and pressing Importance, unless suspended in their Operation till his Assent should be obtained; and when so suspended, he has utterly neglected to attend to them. He has refused to pass other Laws for the Accommodation of large Districts of People, unless those People would relinquish the Right of Representation in the Legislature, a right inestimable to them and formidable to Tyrants only. He has called together Legislative Bodies at Places unusual, uncomfortable, and distant from the Depository of their public Records, for the sole Purpose of fatiguing them into Compliance with his Measures. He has manipulated Representative Houses repeatedly, for opposing with manly Firmness his Invasions on the Rights of The People. He has refused for a long Time, after such Dissolutions, to cause others to be elected; whereby the Legislative Powers, incapable of Annihilation, have returned to The People at large for their exercise; the State remaining in the mean time exposed to all the Dangers of Invasion from without, and Convulsions within. He has endeavored to prevent the Population of these States and its peoples; for that Purpose obstructing the Laws for Naturalization of Foreigners; refusing to pass others to encourage their Migrations hither, and raising the Conditions of new Appropriations of Lands. He has obstructed the Administration of Justice, by refusing his assent to Laws for establishing Judiciary Powers. He has made Judges dependent on his Will alone, for the Tenure of their Offices, and the Amount and Payment of their Salaries.

He has erected a Multitude of new Offices, and sent hither Swarms of Officers to harass our People, and eat out their Substance. He has kept among us, in Times of Peace, Standing Armies, without the consent of our Legislatures. He has affected to render the Military independent of and superior to the Civil Power. He has combined with others to subject us to a Jurisdiction foreign to our Constitution, and unacknowledged by our Laws; giving his Assent to their Acts of pretended Legislation: For quartering large Bodies of Armed Troops among us: For protecting them, by a mock Trial, from Punishment for any Murders which they should commit on the Inhabitants of these States and its peoples: For manipulating our Trade with all Parts of the World: For imposing Taxes on us without our Consent: For depriving us, in many Cases, of the Benefits of Trial by Jury: For transporting us between States to be tried for pretended Offences: For abolishing the free System Laws in a neighboring Province, establishing therein an arbitrary Government, and enlarging its Boundaries, so as to render it at once an Example and fit Instrument for introducing the same absolute Rule into these States: For manipulating our Charters, abolishing our most valuable Laws, and altering fundamentally the Forms of our Governments: For manipulating our own Legislatures, and declaring themselves invested with Power to legislate for us in all Cases whatsoever. He has abdicated pretend Government here, by declaring that he is protecting us and waging War against other Nations. He has plundered our

Seas, ravaged other Nation's Coasts, burnt other Nation's Towns, and destroyed the Lives of other People. He is, at this Time, transporting large Armies of Mercenaries to complete the Works of Death, Desolation, and Tyranny, already begun with circumstances of Cruelty and Perfidy, scarcely paralleled in the most barbarous Ages, and totally unworthy the Head of a civilized Nation. He has constrained our fellow Citizens and from other Nations to bear Arms against other Countries, to become the Executioners of their Friends and Brethren, or to fall themselves by their Hands. He has excited domestic Insurrections amongst us. In every stage of these Oppressions, we have petitioned for Redress in the most humble Terms: Our repeated Petitions have been answered only by repeated Injury. A Prince, whose Character is thus marked by every act which may define a Tyrant, is unfit to be the Ruler of a free People. We must, therefore, acquiesce in the Necessity, which denounces our Separation, and hold them, as we hold the rest of Humans, Enemies in War, in Peace, Friends. We, therefore, the Representatives of *THE AMERICAN REPUBLIC*, in General Congress, Assembled, appealing to the Supreme Judge of the World for the Rectitude of our Intentions, do, in the Name, and by Authority of the good People of these United States of America, solemnly Publish and Declare, That these United States of America and its peoples are, and of Right ought to be a FREE AND INDEPENDENT *AMERICAN REPUBLIC*; that they are absolved from all Allegiance to the current

Government of the United States of America, and that all political

Connection between them and the current Government of the United States

of America, is and ought to be totally dissolved; and that as a FREE AND

INDEPENDENT *AMERICAN REPUBLIC*, they have full Power to levy

War, conclude Peace, contract Alliances, establish Commerce, and to do

all other Acts and Things which an INDEPENDENT *AMERICAN*

REPUBLIC may of right do. And for the support of this Declaration, with a

firm Reliance on the Protection of divine Providence, we mutually pledge

to each other our Lives, our Fortunes, and our sacred Honor.

Opening Statement: raison d'être

Those who understand, decided that the time has come to allow me to

undertake this task to put on paper the ideas and principles for a free and

honest society as seen thru the eyes of one who has been given the

opportunity to witness the future.

It came with a choice to tell the truth, or to continue on the current path of

lies, deceit, and ignorance. My choice was to tell the truth, from my point

of view.

This choice comes with great sacrifice, as do many when one wishes to change the environment in which they live.

In order to incite change, one must have made that change within themselves.

It is very difficult to tell the truth in a society that uses the truth as bait for those who are not aware that there are demons in the forest waiting to devour the innocent.

I am an American Patriot, a human being who has been given a third chance.

This Manifestum is not intended to impress intellectuals, but is rather a Manifestum for all people. It is written in style for all to read and understand. The purpose of this Manifestum is to enlighten those Americans who are truly unhappy with their lives and their government, as it provides for them the choice of welcoming in a new government. This Manifestum will incite those who wish for change for Americans. This change will replace the old government and its organs, with *The American Republic*.

II. *The American Republic*, Common Sense, Virtue

A government must have sole rule over The People it governs, and govern with a strong will. Diplomacy is for Diplomats who take their orders and influence from the government.

Religion, or any other cult, will not have any influence over *The American Republic* government. The absence of religious influence in *The American Republic* government will make it easier to enforce change for the better of the many, and not the few.

Capitalist businesses will not have any influence over *The American Republic* government; government will have influence over Capitalist business. Charter Corporations that serve the Public Trusts will only be allowed and controlled by *The American Republic* government.

People of America will form and control government for the benefit of The People. No longer will the government be influenced by the few who wish to rule with lies and deceit.

The American Republic is a new idea of government for The People of America, and should be adopted as a model to other nations to use as a standard of government.

The American Republic is the Mother and Father of the Homeland; it is the all-seeing, all knowing eye of providence. It is a new order of the Ages. God will have nothing to do with this government.

The American Republic is a government that will eliminate the top-heavy administrations that operate with impunity, as they do under the laws of America's current system of government.

Time will not be expended on explaining the state of affairs, as they exist today, because they are in constant unrest. You can better determine and compare policies and events at the time this document is being read without the fear of radical reprisal.

Your new government will be a new Republic, re-defined correcting the errors of those who misused government to enslave the weak, reward the dishonest, and pacify those duped by it all. It is not in the new Republic's design for people's patriotism to be dismantled and redirected back to the old ways of government.

It is important to understand that birthing a new system of government comes with great sacrifice and some disappointment. Just as a mother slowly forgets the pangs of childbirth in heralding in the newest member of the family, it is expected that people will react similarly to the inception of a new government.

The idea of *The American Republic* is a fresh new approach to governing The People it will serve. It will serve without prejudice and malice towards The People. *The American Republic* is a chance for all Americans to finally experience life under a government that will no longer rule over them with lies and deceit. Fighting back and containing the surge of unchecked corporate business in America is but one of many tasks.

Rewards with substantial income increases to current Military personnel are yet another new government benefit. The new government will clean up the ranks of the cowards and traitors in the current military and have them brought before a newly designed military tribunal, and if found guilty of treasonous crimes, the offending personnel will be severely punished under law. Under *The American Republic law,* there will be no room for treason. All public servants will come under review from the Executive Mansion down, to ferret out the guilty. In addition, when proven in the new Court of Law of their crimes against *The American Republic*, they will be severely punished under law. No jail terms for traitors.

Clandestine organizations connected with the current government of America will also be given a chance to redeem themselves before being brought to trial. Those found guilty will suffer the same fate as any other traitor.

The American Republic will be a government made up of people who live to tell the truth and who believe in helping fellow citizens in need. It is important to note that one American without, is one too many. Poverty and ignorance is not acceptable under the new government of *The American Republic*.

Those who wish to have a society controlled by The People will be those who govern *The American Republic*. The current system of government in America has failed its people because it has moved too far from its original goals and has allowed dishonest people to manage it. *The American Republic* will correct this. It is unfortunate that this change and control must be severe. For two centuries, America's very foundation, as set by the founding fathers, has been systematically torn apart. Americans have become puppets to government puppet masters, who masquerade as saviors of the human freedoms. These charlatans write words of untruths only to appease the masses of those who believe America to be a place of freedom, peace, and harmony. That, however, will not be the practice under the new rule of government. This "beast" has surreptitiously devoured our inherent freedoms and replaced them with counterfeits.

The current socio-economic environment has destroyed America and most of its citizens. There is no other hope than to wash this land clean with something other than their blood.

The current system of government in America has allowed Americans to be without and to suffer so much that apathy and fear has become the norm of the majority. The fortunate have lost their souls to the greed of amassing money, and have cleverly employed that to assume power over others. Real power is not about keeping citizens torn apart, it is instead about encouraging them to come together willingly, with beliefs that are based upon reason and trust. Diversity is encouraged.

The American Republic will give every American, regardless of race, religion, or sexual orientation, an equal opportunity to become whatever they want to be for the survival of the Republic and The People it serves. No, cost is too great to insure our freedoms.

The current system of government is now in shambles and needs replacement. The "Game" that many have played over the last two centuries has evolved into an uncontrollable pandemonium. It is quite apparent just by looking at Americans that they are suffering. Equality is but a dream for so many, but this can and will be achieved with the new government. We must change America first, then hope other Nations can evaluate what we have accomplished, and make a choice to follow the same.

There are thousands of websites, books, clubs, organizations, and even patriots advocating change to the current government and its systems of law. The problem is there are too many solutions leading in too many different directions of thought. It has become a fractal of ideas identified with no leader or leaders who can sort through the maze of beliefs hoping to come to a consensus of reason.

As stated earlier, this Manifestum is not intended to point out the voluminous infractions that have become embedded into our current society. This Manifestum is illuminating a new idea to those who really wish for change for all. *The American Republic* will be designed to listen to the needs of all of The People, not just the privileged, as does the current government.

If you wish to understand what is happening on your planet, or in America, take your head out of the sand; quit blaming others for your Nation's demise. This Manifestum is not intended to be a literary success. It is not written in style just for the learned and is not a detailed philosophical, scientific, or political treatise. It is only a Manifestum miscellany of ideas, principles, and solutions for Americans. It is a Manifestum of truth for anyone, anywhere who wishes to be free, and treated with respect, dignity, and love.

Now let us take a journey in words of action to better understand what The American Republic will do for Americans today and for tomorrow:

A government formed "by The People" must be very vigilant not to tolerate those who have been accustomed to slavery and other inhumane atrocities to obtain even a minute roothold on the new system of law. Replacing the current system of government in America is the direction *The American Republic* plans to move. It has come time to transform current laws to include all citizens. No longer will selfish political leaders benefit from individualized rules of law that usurp the regulations originally designed to govern The People.

Government is both the Mother and Father of the Homeland. Would your parents leave one sibling without? Would a shepherd leave one sheep out of the flock? A reasonable person would answer "no" to both questions. Pause here to take a mental inventory of your current state of affairs to see for yourself what your Government (parents) has done for you. Unless you belong to the outrageously affluent Oligarchy, that make up less than 1% of the American socioeconomic faction, then what you tally will pale in comparison. This gross imbalance of power will not be tolerated or allowed within *The American Republic*. Americans have been duped into believing that it is the rich who should be in power.

America is home to every type of human kind. With that in mind, we must always consider everyone's position. Over 300 million? A good start. We must first regard the positions of all who legally live in America, before considering those who do not. Note: Without question, Native Tribal inhabitants will always be included as living legally in America. They are the first Americans.

America is a wonderful land with vast natural resources. The most valuable of these resources, as mentioned, supra, include humans. Nature has always displayed an inherent way of balancing itself to maintain the natural order of living things. Particles of matter include all the forces that bind and unbind substances, all working together to create the "soup" of "living" objects in the universe.

We are but a miniscule element of this vast infinite never-ending chronicle that folds and unfolds in perpetuity. There is no "until." God and religion are merely interpretations of the beginning of a human's sophomoric understanding of human and earth's relationship to the sun (star). Just as this planet has evolved while orbiting the sun, so have humans. All living things on earth continue to evolve as the result of this universal revolution created by energy (aether) working together to embrace this wonderful dance of nature that affords earth's transformation.

Everything we know, as experienced through our many senses are but a small part of the whole of nature. The feeble and antiquated technologies that humans hold so dear are but a shadow of triumph as compared to nature's wonders. Moreover, like clockwork, within a millennium all will eventually be turned under into the earth's mountainous heaps of long-forgotten debris, just as a farmer tills under old crops for new.

Thus, until enlightened, we will continue to ask who are we? What is our purpose? How shall we live? How shall we eat? What do we believe to be our religion (way of life)? How do we love one another? Why and how shall we be governed?

There are billions of answers and points of views that can entertain these simple questions interpreting them in such a way that total agreement will be nearly impossible. This leads to confusion of the masses, and such confusion leads to effortless manipulation. Hence, the age-old trick of governments.

Now that technology has progressed to storage in Exabyte's and speed in Exaflops, nearly every human on this planet can be impacted by information that can enlighten, enslave, deceive, and control. These present crucial daily choices we make seek the Natural Order.

We, as humans, are designed to be able to adapt or take control, like all other living things on this planet, making us no different from any other organism that exists. In this "move over or be taken over" model, humans believe they have been given the upper hand in the world, and it is by this fact alone that they feel they possess the power to conquer, control, destroy, create, and share in the establishment of what exists. This concept has become the exemplary followed that has made our world in their image. Moreover, it is in this world where humans continually live under the rule of these misguided governments.

A select minority of humans to control other humans through words created government. We must forge ahead with our senses and pretend that we know where we are going, even though we have no idea of where we have been. Humans were set forth on missions by their government leaders to reap knowledge like crops, and then given orders whether or not to share some, all or none of this bounty with their community (family). Imparting that knowledge is for those who are part of the selective community, and who consider themselves the sum of the whole. The consequences of our actions and choices, however, are evident today. Life is not as precious to our government as we imagine. Using a mix of philosophy and religion these leaders convince and influence the many through words and violence; an effective coercion for eons. Using human emotions has been another effectual tool to control others. Humans began to understand each other the day they crawled from under the rocks of ignorance and fear, and it was at that moment that humans discovered the chink in the armor. It took some time for humans to learn to understand their survival instinct, but it was instantaneously curtailed by fear of reprisal by lawmakers. Fear is a disease; do not let it into your heart.

Human evolution, as influenced by the Yin and Yang of the changing electromagnetic field of the earth, coupled by outside intervention from extraterrestrials, has allowed humans to evolve into a species quite different in character from other beings. It took an event of epic proportions to disrupt the ecosystem when it replaced the Jurassic creatures with flora and fauna naturally selected by Natures wisdom. Humans survived over millions of years by natural selection and help from other beings which finally got them to a point of self-governance, only to be faced in the 21st century with the looming extinction of their freedoms and lives.

The earth will remain earth long after humans have become dust in the wind. As with government, it too, will suffer the same fate if allowed to continue, unchecked.

Misinterpretations can be dangerous if believed by too many who have been mislead by false words. As stated before, words are a very powerful tool that can be used as a weapon, tactic, or both. Humans interpret based on beliefs, truth and deceit. Their choices ultimately determine the fate of planet earth and all its inhabitants.

The symbol for *The American Republic* is the Great Seal of the current government of America:

Symbolism has been used throughout the ages to identify and signify the intent and power of its purpose. *The American Republic* will use the same symbols that are presently in use by the current government of America.

These symbols will be used to identify those who are loyal to the new government of America.

All who use these symbols will be recognized as those who are true to the government, and only that government. Any fraudulent use of these symbols used for other nefarious purposes will be punishable by the laws of *The American Republic*.

We will explain *The American Republic* Governmental platform for North America throughout this discourse.

Before any revolution can take place, the rules and expected outcome must be defined for all to understand. Making a choice to replace a government is not an easy decision to make, but it must be made when there are millions suffering under its governance. A carefully orchestrated non violent COUP *d'état* will have to occur if there are any hopes of replacing the current government in America. A successful implementation of this tactic is the only way, short of a civil war, to bring about real change for every American everywhere without regard to any social pre-qualifier. Collective representation seems to be the dominant qualifier for Americans under the current American government, all defined by social and money status. The current constitution already gives the authority to The People to change.

The American Republic will also require the formation of a Continental Congress composed of citizens from every State and Territory of America, to join in solidarity to resolve differences and generate innovative ideas for successful laws and programs dedicated to improving the Homeland for all. Such a meeting can be held in any state of America. When a new draft of a Constitution is finished, then it will be presented to all of The People of America who will decide by vote, on any new government for America. The target date is December 21, 2012.

There will be a complete reorganization of the current government in America, with relevant new rules, titles and responsibilities, and most importantly, accountability.

The American Republic will stress that Religion will have no place with government, thus it will not be considered when forming a new government or laws for America.

"I pledge allegiance to my Flag and the Republic for which it stands; one Nation indivisible, with Liberty and Justice for all."- Francis Bellamy

III.   Military, *The American Republic* Army, Way of Tea

Strong, well-trained, and well-financed armed forces are the only sure way that an entering body of government can effectively and efficiently replace the current ruling class. The current armed forces in America have generally been mislead, mistreated and undercompensated since the first Continental Army was formed in the 1700's. In the new government, every solider will be compensated with full benefits of pay and insurance for themselves and their families, regardless of rank or years of service. It is obvious that there are but a few officers who are mentally and financially content at the higher-ranking levels, but then there are millions at lower class and grade levels who are not. The new government will bring much needed reform to military.   Some civilians and some military personnel making up the current Pentagon administration are not there for the best interests of our Nation, our Homeland. This will be remedied. The American Veterans who sacrificed life and limb in defense of this Nation are still being treated, as outcasts without hope not long after they return home. Even now, the current system of government leaves them jobless, homeless, or languishing away in lonely Veterans Administration facilities, with little hope of relief. For the rare few who are taken care of, that care is merely satisfactory and not commensurate with their valor in protecting America.

Every solider will live a good life without any struggle for funds. The "spoils of war" will be spread to every soldier, regardless of rank or time served. Celebrity status will be awarded to all soldiers, past, present, and future. No soldiers will be homeless in the new government. Those who are sick, living on a fixed income, convalescing, or suffering from addictions under the current government, will find immediate relief from *The American Republic* Government. Soldiers will be recognized as great warriors. Their willingness to sacrifice their lives so that others can live is the greatest gift anyone can give. Soldiers will be helped without regard to rank and file. The current Veterans Administration, including hospitals, will be drastically upgraded to offer the same treatment as would be offered the President of *The American Republic*. When seeing a Veteran or a current American Republic Army soldier, we will stand in respect and acknowledge their service to the *American Republic* in keeping us safe and from harm's way.

Under the new government, it will be required that all citizens respect every solider of every rank of service and treat them as the heroes they are, without prejudice. There will be no more disrespect given to any *American Republic* army soldier. If that occurs, there will be a severe punishment placed on the offender.

On their 22nd birthday, all Americans, male and female, will be required to enlist in military service for 3 years. After the 3 years of compulsory service, enlistees will have the choice of either continuing their service up to retirement at age 62 or opting for a government-supported compulsory educational program of required training for a Degree or Certification in a chosen field of study.

It is very important that when advocating a non violent *coup d'état,* the entire military of America understands that there is only one-way to go and that is on the side of The People. To take any other side would be considered treasonous against the American people and the government of *The American Republic.*

The current military in America has many great soldiers, but unfortunately soldiers who are not so great have poorly managed it. The new Congress will reorganize the entire Armed Services to better its domestic and global functions. All military, as well as, non-government personnel will be re-evaluated before re-drafting them into the new Armed Forces service. Loyalty without the fear of death will be a primary prerequisite for service in the Armed Forces, and to *The American Republic.* Anything less will not qualify.

The American Republic Army will be broken down into various military components.

The President and his/her select cabinet will be trained in the art of war and leadership. If war is waged, the President and his/her staff will move to a protected front to coordinate and defend the Homeland along with the

Armed Forces and their ranked leaders.

The President will be the true "commander and chief." The President along with his/her staff will not display cowardice and must be willing to be the first to fight, the last to leave, and the first to die for the protection of the freedoms of *The American Republic*. A Sheppard does not run from his/her flock when danger is eminent, the Sheppard will stand and defend the flock, even if death is the outcome.

The President is not the government. Under the new government, the Congress of The People is the government. *The American Republic* Congress will always be defining the law of the land. The President, Congress and all Public servants will be there to serve The People, not the other way around.

The military will have the best battle technology available. The newest technology will always be used to defend our governmental interests. It is of primary importance that our soldiers be well-protected and only used in combat as a precursor to the final solution: complete annihilation of the enemy. Our military is not enlisted to defend the business interests of private investors or corporate moguls; they are

to defend the interests of *The American Republic* and its people.

We call on the Armed Forces of America to come to our aid and stand with us to restore what is rightfully ours and yours. Remember your families if you have any are still The People. As for Rules of Engagement, they will have to be rewritten for the times.

IV. Religion

Religion has been the source of much discord on this planet for eons, and it is well understood that religion continues to play a central role in decision making in most governments. Business and private affairs, be it by oracle, divine intervention, extraterrestrial, falsehood promise, messianic promise, or any other pagan thought are key influences of the world's religious belief systems. Preying on government elected official's religious sensitivities, a reverend influenced the inclusion of "*IN GOD WE TRUST*," to be inscribed on American currency in the late 1860s, so that people would not view America as a *heathen nation*. However, which *God* are these inscriptions referring? Is it the God who is the masterful propagandist, the warrior, the destroyer, the racist, the lover, the hater, or the egotist? Do you want that God to be representative of your government? There will be no mention of any God or any religion on *American Republic* text, symbols, or any other government property. Religion will have no influence or special considerations in government with *The American Republic*.

The non-profit tax status will be removed from all religious enterprises, and replaced with a for profit tax status; this will be the new business code for all religious ventures and their respective empires. These business enterprises will be taxed as any other for profit business, with penalties and levies attached. There will be no corporate veil, shelter, or other financial scheme to hide behind for any religion under the new government. Religion will move back to its original intent, worshiping in community sanctuaries and following all laws of *The American Republic*, without compromise.

Citizens of *The American Republic* will be loyal and will respect the government of *The American Republic* first, with family second, and religion, last. God has no place in *The American Republic*.

Human Beings fear of the unknown and the appalling thought of being in complete isolation have forced humans to seek out mysterious life forces, other than the sun to guide them. This human intervention has so rapidly evolved into the religious belief systems sprouting up around the planet. God is but a creation of human's alter ego, and this celestial intervention has only led to morbid distortions of humans search for his or her God. Religion is ultimately the root of all the evils existing in the world. Even though it professes good, history has already documented the paradoxes of religion and the hypnotic hold it maintains on those who seek its wonder. Nature is the only true God to reign over humans. Humans fear what they cannot understand, thus the creation of something greater than one's self. God remains an elusive and nebulous myth, created by humans to replace their devotion to the sun. Allegorical chronicles have been assembled to carry on the never-ending quest for some entity greater than one's self.

V. Government, Oligarchy

Government has also been a major source of dissension on this planet. It has triggered the genocide of populations, as well as, the extinction of many of earth's flora and fauna.

There is voluminous data that can be found on the current American government's contradictory philosophies for change and control. Keeping The People confused and conflicted controls their recognition of the truth. This is the same government, while outwardly resolute in its commitment to protect and serve The People, governs instead with fabrication and treachery. However, America has lost its stars and stripes in the dirt it ultimately stirred up with the continual betrayal of its citizens.

In *The American Republic*, every person will have a voice that will be heard. America is a collective of people from all lifestyles and its citizens will always be encouraged to share ideas and express themselves freely without fear of reprisal. America has not lived up to the promises made to its citizens, thus the current state of affairs. Again, we can all research the existing state of the union to find the never-ending ball of twine the government is wrapping us in.

How will *The American Republic* be organized? A Congress of people will be assembled from every part of America. Elections will be held in each pre-determined district by a reliable election process. Qualifications will be determined by ideas and merit, not by money or influence.

Nationalization of all of America's natural resources will be essential to the success of *The American Republic* Government. Key business resources will also be nationalized under the new government. In order for the strength of government to be realized, it must be the sole proprietor of all vital resources. The current governmental leaders and their immediate followers will be replaced with loyal government compatriots. Current government departments will be reorganized to comply totally with the new government's mandates and philosophies. Any government official found to be out of step with the new protocols will either be counseled or eliminated. All workers, from mid-management to the core will be evaluated for work ethics and loyalty.

Senatorial seats will be eliminated, for they are yet another corrupt level of government. Clandestine agencies will be left intact for they will be an integral part of *The American Republic*'s National Security. However, they too, will also be held accountable and will be expected to maintain unconditional loyalty to the new government.

All states of the current union will lose all legislative powers. The office of the governor will be the sole regulator of the state taking orders from the *American Republic* government. Central government will be the new order for America. That is why it is very important that this central government of, by, and for The People work together, as one. This central government will eliminate wastefulness of the time and energy that so many Americans loathe.

The resources that are held by each state will be evenly distributed to each other so that all Americans can benefit from each other. Any deficiencies accounted for will be corrected by resource re-allocation. No state of *The American Republic* will ever have to suffer from having not. Business will no longer be allowed to flourish under religious law. The un American zealots infesting every corner of government will be eliminated.

Every citizen of *The American Republic* will be required to have a properly shielded electronic device surgically implanted into his or her right or left hand, or forehead. This device will contain virtually all personal and financial data about that citizen, from birth. The latest technology will be employed in the design of these devices, which includes a Global Positioning Tracking System. This digital instrument will be a crucial element in the elimination of crimes against citizens of *The American Republic*. All transactions, purchases, sales, or services made by, between, or with citizens, be it with or without expressed permission, will be recorded to these devices. This will deter the embezzling, fraud, theft, shoplifting, swindles, cons, etc., against citizens. Only commerce entities legally registered with *The American Republic* will have limited access to the codes required to complete authorized business transactions, and those are the only codes that will be made available to them. When a device wears out or its technology is to be upgraded, each citizen will be required to replace or update accordingly. This electronic device will remain with each person from birth to death. Upon a citizen's death, the implant will be securely stored in the Hall of Digital Records. *The American Republic* will have full control of the system and/or systems that monitors these devices. A Digital Forensics branch of government will be established, and charged with the secure monitoring of Americans' safety.

In order for government to give protection to its people, it must know everything there is to know. Under the current American government, this would be considered an "invasion of privacy," but Americans have had their privacies quietly invaded for centuries by their so-called Democratic government. *The American Republic* will protect the privacy of its citizens at all costs.

To the religious zealots who bark at this new order of watchful protection, let them claim the coming of their "messiahs." They will never be able to negotiate or alter what is to be. This new world order will demonstrate to the millions of believers of their faiths that the end of times was only a children's tale, a myth.

One world government is a means to an end. People of America have become so apathetic to their lives and to the true purpose of a government that they have signed over to those who know the truth, the keys to the proverbial kingdom. This ignorance has cost citizens of America, their power, which has been the case since they first began turning away from reality.

The freedoms guaranteed by the original Manifestum, called the Constitution, will obviously be redefined to accommodate the society of today.

Freedom of Speech will mean to all citizens of *The American Republic* that they are free to say whatever they want without fear of reprisal. There will be no violent reprisals for the honest spoken word. If violence results, it will not be tolerated.

The current Supreme Court of America and the respective state counterparts are mockeries of justice; managed by vampires called lawyers and succubae called judges.

America's system of law will be re-evaluated by the new Congress, and the citizens will have the right and honor to analyze the final rules of law before ratification.

The American government has become so unstable that the only hope for a secure future for its citizens is reformation. Once the current governmental powers realize this new course of action is imminent and their reign is over, citizens will unite if they are to guarantee a swift eradication.

A government by The People and for The People is the only way that a community of people can exist in these times. Those who have plenty are not willing to share, and those who have not would like to share if they could. America is too great a nation to let even one of its own suffer in hunger or despair.

As for weapons, guns and the like, current laws have stripped Americans of their right to bear arms. Disappearing is the self-respect citizens feel when protecting their Homeland from invaders. However, the current laws have become so convoluted and uncontrollable that bearing arms under the original interpretation is impossible. If *The American Republic* is to insure the safety of all American citizens, the only viable solution will be the removal of all weapons from The People.

Trusting in the Government and its Military to protect the Homeland will be the only way that Americans will give up their Arms. Trust is earned. All local law enforcement entities will report to a Policing Department within *The American Republic*. This new branch's sole responsibility will be to maintain law and order within every state of *The American Republic*. They will maintain accountability for the protection of every citizen. Private mercenary or vigilante forces will not operate under color of law anywhere in the territories of *The American Republic*. Their organization will never be authorized. If *The American Republic* Government does not live up to its promises, then it is the right of The People to make change by any means necessary. Any person or persons found conspiring to organize or rise against *The American Republic* for unethical reasons, will suffer swift justice.

Congress will have the power to keep order and make laws, while the

President will be the sole decision maker on passing all laws coming from Congress. The People who are chosen to be members of Congress will be those who are not afraid to die for their beliefs, are driven to tell the truth, are willing to make sacrifices for *The American Republic*, have the common sense to know right from wrong, possess the ability to reason, and have learned from their past transgressions. The President must also be of the same character. No longer will wealth and political influence be the tacit requirements for leaders. Common sense with a good mix of reason will do. All members of government, including those making up the Judicial Branches, must also be of the same in character. However, the one edge the President must have over all others is the ability to govern as a benevolent dictator, with a warrior's instinct. This leader must be one who still possesses a willingness to be truthful and just. The president must be willing to give up his or hers life for The People of the Homeland.

It is no secret that the current system of government is not working well for Americans, and that it must be completely replaced with a new one. The People who wish to be in control of any proposed Government must operate on a philosophy that is agreed upon by them all.

A civil government whose leaders have truly been elected by The People will be the one that earns the public trust. Anything less than that is what ultimately exists in America today.

There has been much speculation about Extraterrestrials. Extraterrestrial visitations will remain under watchful eye until the word is given to disclose. It is very important that information about our current relationships and technology exchanges with the Extraterrestrials remain undisclosed, until properly gleaned and evaluated. Protective measures will be in place to ensure against premature disclosures, because the resulting implications to the world would be chaotic and not in the best interests of National or worldwide security.

The current system of money exchange will be re-evaluated. A fiat system, or any other for that fact, has not proven to be beneficial for the whole of whom it was intended to serve. America's current Federal Reserve System is a failure to its people and will be replaced with a new system of exchange under *The American Republic*. In short, a central bank of government will be the only way to guarantee the proper management of some sort of debit and credit system for the exchange of goods and services. So that the central bank retains continuous knowledge of locations, transactions, or exchanges, all paper and coin currency, bank notes, stock certificates, credit/debit devices, etc., will have RFID Nano chip technology embedded. The Digital Forensics branch of the government will assist the central bank in secure data tracking, retrieval, and recovery. The Central Bank and its state satellites will exchange current currencies, in like values, for the new. Once these exchanges are complete, citizens will no longer be able to buy or sell with the old currencies and means of exchange. All monies and transactions will become electronic.

Too many people have little and too few have more. This imbalance of wealth will change. All Americans must be allowed to benefit from the wealth that this great Nation has to offer its citizens.

Taxes are contributions made by those to finance a system of government. The People through their Congress will decide on this. There of course will be several types of tax contributions made by The People who labor for commerce, and by businesses that buy and sell goods for commerce. There will be no more State Tax of any kind. All taxes collected will be evaluated by each state's annual commerce income.

Sovereignty is fundamental to the autonomy of each state, and this independence will be respected and protected.

Having a central government controlling the majority of affairs is the only way to ensure financial stability and security to each state of the Republic. A state will no longer compete with other states, but only with itself in its efforts to improve the lifestyles of its citizens.

Nationalization will be the only way that America will survive into the next century. Without it, America would decline into a Nation, with an uncontrolled, unchecked system fraught with capitalist opportunists. Well-planned programs will have to be created to manage the wealth of ideas American citizens possess. A massive continental reconstruction plan will be one of the first programs to be initiated. This model will be of the same purpose as was the building of the great pyramids whose very design respected the geological and astrological forces on this planet. The cities of America are so poorly designed that they can never be beneficial to the earth's environment. The entire landscape of America will have to be redeveloped. This development may take decades, and will require that every American become trained in one or more skills essential to this renovation.

Every American citizen will have a home and enough land to put it on. Farming will be a priority. No more unregulated genetically engineered products will be distributed for human consumption for mere financial gain, and consumer is damned. Unless it can be unequivocally proven that such scientifically altered items will only benefit the end user, all financial support to such public and private research centers will cease. Grain/seed and fertilizer companies and moneylenders will no longer hold farmer's fields hostage, or profit from deceitful schemes. Commerce will release its stronghold on the livestock, poultry, and fish industries, and central government will be in control of the health and safety regarding processing and packaging conditions. The current profit margin has become so blurred by greed that commerce has lost sight of who it was designed to benefit. Under the new system, the consumer and the consumer's health and welfare will come first. There will be a balance of farming for animals. The goal of course is a meatless consuming society.

Through this massive reconstruction project, every American will have employment. *The American Republic* will provide the training, supplies, and education, for its citizens, with pay (to scale).

There will be no more poor and homeless citizens in America. Wealth can and will be divided in such a way that all Americans will have plenty.

The current system of government has been corrupt since its inception, which has resulted in the disorder America finds itself in today. Of course those individuals, corporations, and religious entities that have amassed wealth, land and influence will share with the Homeland what they have accumulated.

Americans have lost their way by choice and selective coercion. America's current system of government has forsaken the poor, the helpless, the sick, the weak, the oppressed, the humbled, and the strong. If one American is without, that is one too many. Money will not decide a person's worth in America. The temptation of financial gain will not be allowed to influence any *American Republic* official. If so, then the severest punishment will be laid upon those persons who have become disloyal.

It is vital that a strong government be formed, so that it can correct the mistakes and crimes committed that have occurred for so long against the American people.

America is in so much disarray, that it is important for the new government to be given complete control over all of its citizens by The People. This control will remain until all who have been corrupt have been eliminated. Millions of lives have been directly affected for decades by the unfair rules and inequitable enforcement of the laws by the self-serving citizens in charge. Instead of living for the American dream, they chase after the flash of riches and fame. The providence that was sought was only an illusion to deceive those who wished to have faith in the Annuit Copetis.

Taxes or Levies are excessive burdens on people, but are necessary for a Nation to function. While State taxes will cease, National taxation will be reinstituted under fair and reasonable regulations. Multiple taxes will end. An *American Republic* tax will be the only national tax an individual or family will be responsible for. Taxes will be based on earned income from goods and services. Export and import taxes will be decided on by a consensus of The People, and must be voted into law by Congress.

There are too many rules regarding the collection of taxes. Every system of collection will be reviewed, and in most cases eliminated if found to contradict the philosophies of *The American Republic*. It is an honor to be a participant in the continuation of a Nation. Adding unnecessary burdens to The People will only harden their hearts and eventually reduce the Nation again to a system of the rich and poor, and haves and haves not. Any more than that will have to be decided on by Congress. Individual

States will work together to build a nation of one. E Pluribus Unum

VI. Environment

Our planet is our home. It is the only home for all living things, as well as, to others not originally from earth. Humans have learned through the ages of all the wonderful resources that the earth has produced to make it habitable.

Leaders in governments and commerce have taken our planet's resources and shattered the intended purpose of nature's gifts. These gross misrepresentations have led to our planet's critical ecological crisis. Earth's air, water, and soil have all been grossly polluted with the wasteful by- products of an inconsiderate commerce. Their genetically and molecularly engineered materials have been released into the earth's bio-structure causing a chain reaction that is now affecting every living thing that relies on earth's resources for life. Humans have always had a propensity to engage in conflict. Even when the indigenous peoples originally inhabiting America were in conflict with each other, they still managed to maintain balance with and respect for earth's natural resources. The earth is itself a living organism that responds to, and in some cases reacts, to input from outside forces. The results are becoming catastrophic and perhaps irreversible. As a counter-reaction, our planet is beginning to release natural defenses to hinder human's path of destruction. Earth will remain in its rotation around the sun until that star completes its life cycle. By that time, humans either will have left to colonize other planets, or will have been naturally selected to become extinct. In America, our government has been as guilty as all others in deciding the fate for the many inhabitants of this planet. These worldwide political systems have allowed business leaders to severely exploit the natural gifts this planet has offered, and this has become an abomination.

Our environment and our planet have always been directly affected by everything we do. Every step we make, every breath we take, every spoken word, every physical action we do has had an effect on the entire bio-system of planet earth.

WE are out of step with nature, thus our dis-ease with earth.

Laws have no real affect on repairing the environment that is humans charge. Our environment has been continually re-adjusting itself for survival. The government of *The American Republic* will not allow any more destruction of the environment. It will truly find, ways to improve and recreate technologies that will work seamlessly with the earth's environment and its inhabitants. *The American Republic* will not take into account the business plans or the profit and loss margins of commerce. It will only be concerned with safeguarding our priority, earth. We will start saving the planet in America, and our successes will serve as an example to the rest of the world. Those countries that continue on the same path of devastation will be shamed into change, for everyone must work towards saving the planet. And if shaming them does not work, then a more direct

---

force of will be implemented.

The United Nations will either help in this cause, or be reorganized or disbanded.

The fates of our civilizations are in the decisions we are making today and tomorrow.

We will never allow the few to leave us homeless. All things living on this planet are depending on us to re-navigate from a dismal future.

It will undoubtedly take a few earth years for the planet to get back in tune with itself, thus the emphasis on the immediacy of government change. With the current rate of resource abuse, humans are rapidly moving into global extinction. Those few making up the minority of humans wishing to continue on the same suicidal path will be ferreted out and eliminated. The real terrorists we must focus on and crush are those that are willfully destroying our planet. The so-called war on terror is right in our backyard, in our America. The government of *The American Republic* will pass enforceable laws on the environment that will help correct the mistakes made in the past, present and in the future. It will work with all peoples to develop new technologies and processes to correct environmental damages. All life is precious and each deserves to live out its life cycle as was intended. Fortunately, there are others from distant civilizations sharing in our same sentiment. There remain many eclectic resources yet to be released for humankind's use. They have been purposefully kept from most humans. If these final resources are discovered too soon and misused, it could accelerate the eventual fate of human life on this planet. Fortunately, those secrets remain under the protection of those with more celestial interests in the future of this planet.

Earth's environment, for now, is our home. With the help from the new government and its greatest resource, its people, America will begin the task of stabilizing our planet. This will be first for Americans, and eventually for the rest of our world. If wars are to be waged, they will be waged not for territory and resources, but for the protection and improvement of our planet's ecology and environment.

VII.   Science and Technology

Science is discovery. Technology is the result of the science of discovery.
For centuries, humans have been curious about their home. From their own
inner intuition and from outside influences, human have evolved thru trial
and error on a wonderful path of dreams.

Every human has in their possession, great gifts, that when ignited by some
inner force yield fantastic results. Formal education is not necessarily the
means required to ignite these gifts. Humans have built in mechanisms
allowing them creative thought, and it is this thought that gives them the
ability to shape reality. The mind is powerful enough to produce spoken
and written word, while painting the spatial patterns of our universe. It is
this thought, coupled with human genetics that has given us our distinct
edge with nature. We do not have the power of nature's full brilliance, but
we have been privy to a very small particle of its magnificence.

The American Republic recognizes the importance of science and
technology and its role in the forward development of the human race.
Without thought, humans would remain in a cauldron of ignorance.
Every American is a scientist in some way, a technologist of sorts.
Americans will be given the opportunity to be recognized for their
thoughts and their contributions to the world of science and technology.
Through a well-planned system of learning, the government will be able to
glean from the population all of the ideas. This will assure the continued

improvement and development of science and technology in America. All things considered, America possesses a small piece of the technological puzzle. The remaining pieces are spread amongst the rest of the planet. It is unnecessary for this Manifestum to explain the various scientific and technological discoveries made over the centuries for that information can be obtained from many sources.

The government of *The American Republic* will designate resources to develop scientific programs that foster growth and development of fresh new ideas: ideas that will take us from the Dark Ages and thrust us all into the Light Ages. All business interests that have a technology base that affects our National Security will be absorbed under the new government. Private enterprise has proven that self-serving interests are the primary objective with the current developers of technology. Nationalizing technology concerns, private labs, and schools of learning will be the only way to guarantee to Americans, that we will be the leaders of technology and science.

It is extremely important that all discoveries, no matter how small or seemingly insignificant, be evaluated. In addition, if found worthy, these innovations will be funded and developed. No approved project will go without the proper funding and support it needs to come to fruition. There will always be protection given to all inventions and discoveries. The government will have full possession of all technologies, thus the elimination of private control and exploitation to the masses of people who can benefit from any technological improvements.

The People of America will be the sole benefactor of all technological achievements developed.

Outer and inner space exploration will be a primary project for development. Antiquated technologies will not be used, approved, or even considered. Land vehicle technology, aircraft technology, fuel technology, power technology, communications technology, warfare technology, environmental technology, education technology, medical technology, metals technology, and any other newly discovered technology will have priority.

Travelers from the universe have, over time, come to our planet for many reasons. Some have even taken residence on earth, and some have used earth as a lab, of sorts. Some have influenced the indigenous inhabitants of earth, and some have given our technology a nudge. These traveler's technologies have existed on earth for eons. The few who have protected this technology as best they can, will know when to release it for human use. For now, however, it is being kept from those who wish to use it as a means to control and murder the innocent.

If knowledge of the past and of the future is disclosed to the public, irreversible changes will be made throughout the domestic and international socioeconomic community. There is a common understanding among a select group of people who understand the grave potential for the scientific, religious, and governmental shock that could result from premature dissemination or thoughtless use of this protected information.

VIII.   Foreign Policy

It is a known fact that America has been infiltrated by many foreign entities masquerading as business leaders, philanthropists, saviors, diplomats, and many other mask-wearing deceivers. This invasion has allowed most of America's land and ideas to be sold off to the highest bidders so that countries outside our borders own more than citizens of this great Nation. A select few Americans have allowed our Nation to become the bastard and whore for the world. Our government has allowed business leaders and other government factions to open our gates to the hoards of devouring demons. What citizens do not realize is that America's commerce, financial holdings, and real property is slowly being swallowed up by these countries. A majority of America is not even ours anymore. Fortunately, money exchange is but a tool that can be eliminated with an electronic system. All current property owned by foreign entities will be under the direct control of *The American Republic*. Foreign ownership of American Property will not be allowed. A fair market price will be offered to all foreign owners of any property in America. Any refusal will be met with seizure of all assets, period   Only American's will be permitted ownership of real property in America, and only after intense scrutiny.

Embassies will be relegated to areas selected by the government of *The American Republic*. Strict rules of diplomacy will be re-established. The

United Nations will have to be overhauled and the North Atlantic Treaty Organization, the same. No longer will foreign ambassadors and the like be able to flagrantly skirt American laws under the color of diplomatic immunity. There will be consequences, fines, imprisonment, and executions instead of slaps on the wrists. *The American Republic* and Congress will solicit input from The People of America. This new alliance will ultimately decide the new rules of diplomacy.

Current wars and conflicts being waged in countries that have American involvement will now be evaluated based on the best interests of *The American Republic* and its citizens. If it is found that the interests do not comply with *American Republic* policy, then America's involvement in that conflict will end, thus leaving the warring Nation to fend on its own. Any outside intervention by any other Nation against *The American Republic* after operations have ceased will be dealt with undiplomatically. The interests of *The American Republic* will always preside.

The current geo-political relationships established under the current American government administration will also be assessed. This evaluation will determine which philosophy of diplomacy will be used to maintain peace and stability in the world.

There are many wars and conflicts being waged, worldwide. Only a few truly understand why these entities are in violent discord. Lives are being lost because of religious differences, pride, greed, and prejudice.

Diplomacy as we understand it has run its course. There are two factions at work, government, and commerce, and both do not mix well. This uncommon bond has created a vacuum in the system of civil peace. There are many nations of people ruled by those with selfish interests who position their personal needs ahead of the needs of The People. Business interests and Politian's get along like two peas in a pod. As long as there is corruption and war, both parties are happy. The resources and funds generated from both are staggering in scale. Conflict is as a big a business as is diplomacy. The current American government is so intertwined with dishonest people that it has become nearly impossible to see beyond their subterfuge. Americans have been so led astray by these charlatans that they have lost complete sight of any feasible governmental philosophy. Americans know not what path to take, and this pleases their current government and business leaders. Citizens are force-fed endless chatters of rhetoric on syndicated news outlets owned by the very ones who are corrupt. This information is passed on as truth when in fact most of it is not. There are no authentic and independent fact finders. Almost everyone in diplomacy is on the take. Big business and the government are ravenous, and America's citizens are on the menu. Nevertheless, it does not stop there. Citizens of other countries are in the crosshairs, as well. NO ONE will be safe until this Nation is restored.

To point out specific nations that are in conflict with the current government of America is not necessary in this document.

It is the philosophy of *The American Republic* that foreign involvement should only occur if an outside nation is at an impasse with another. If natural resources are threatened by misuse and management, if some sort of tyrannical rule will also oppress the freedoms of a people, if mindless rule breeds discord beyond that Nation, if some other nation invades without just cause, or any other situation that threatens to impede the natural growth and prosperity of a nation, then and only then will *The American Republic* see fit to interfere and re-establish balance for that nation and its people.

A key indicator that a problem exists with foreign policy is evident by the shameless lack of concern for the respective Nation's citizens. This is uncovered when countless heinous crimes are uncovered after the dust of their frivolous conflicts settle.

The United Nations and its organs are in complete disarray. This body and its members have not lived up to the original charter of promise, and until its principles are redirected to truly benefit of the world's citizens, as was designed, *The American Republic* will not participate.

The North Atlantic Treaty Organization is another disorganized farce that needs to be reformed. *The American Republic* Armed Forces will not participate in this body until such time that all offenders have been ferreted out and punished like the criminals they are. This tactic will also apply to members of the United Nations.

As mentioned earlier in this document, once in power, *The American Republic* will resolve its differences with foreign entities that seek revenge for our involvement in curtailing their instigated conflicts.

American Republic Armed Forces will be pulled back in strategic numbers and reassigned to the borders of America. Those troops assigned to remain in foreign locations will be placed in key tactical positions to keep the peace until stabilization of the entire nation has been established.

Troops will be rotated every six (6) months to give them an opportunity to spend time with their families. Congress will determine leave time for the Armed Forces of *The American Republic*.

A new foreign policy enacted upon by Congress will resolve any issues currently under duress. This policy will take into account the already strained relations between America and its neighbors. It will be a strong direct policy that does not mix words, a policy that will be well written and well understood. Most importantly, it will not be susceptible to self-serving interpretations.

It is well understood that every nation admits to some interest in other countries. When this is mixed with deceit, the only possible outcome for that targeted Nation is disruption, exploitation, and eventual takeover. Our current government imposes restrictions on offending nations in the form of embargos and other covert operations to cutoff the lifeline of a nation to force eventual submission. That is not the way to solve differences. The planet is finite in size and can adequately accommodate all of its inhabitants with room and resources to spare. It takes the elimination of egos to be able to effectively support a common planet, and just learn to get along with others of like kind.

IX. Education, Polymathēs

 Knowledge is the key to understanding one's place in the universe. It is one of many ways that a human can keep from regressing. Wisdom is a means to the success of any Nation and its people.

All educational systems will be under the direct control of a department of *The American Republic*. No more state or local control. No more wasteful management of the students learning.

Funding will never be an issue to education. The cost of educating our citizens will be covered under the America Republic's education program. No, out of pocket expenses will be required for any American who wishes to, or is required to attend an educational facility or campus.

A well-informed society will do well with others.

All colleges of education, private and public, will come under direct control of a department of *The American Republic*.

All educators who are directly involved in the teaching of citizens will be one of the most compensated of any other trade or service. They will be treated with dignity and respect at all times. No one is greater than a teacher is, for without a guide how does one find his or her way? Without teachers, you have no professions or professionals to run them. Teachers are the primary component in the success of any community or nation. Education and experience are one in the same, without them both you have a society that can be controlled. A good teacher is one who comes to students with life experiences, as well as, an education.

Congress will be responsible to develop educational curriculum for all Americans, and assign responsibilities to those who will manage the new educational system.

Every American, regardless of age, race, or gender, will have the opportunity to become educated in the field of their abilities.

Compulsory education will be required from a pre-determined age until completion of a 4-year post-secondary degree and/or certificated training program.

If one desires to continue on to master a discipline, then that option can be exercised.

Education is a tool to be integrated into the nation.

No students in the compulsory program will be eligible for employment, for this will only distract from their educational studies.

All needs will be provided to citizens enrolled in compulsory education. A parent or guardian is free to supplement any additional expenses but it will not be needed or required.

All educational courses and respective curriculums will be designed with input from the American people. However, based on that input their Congress will ultimately decide what courses will be in the best interest of the Homeland. No religious belief systems will influence or have any bearing on what courses will prevail. Religion has its place, and it is not in the educational structure. Religious history will be taught in the educational system only. Religious educational facilities will not be permitted or even recognized as legal educational systems. However, religions can teach their philosophy while in their buildings of faith. There will be a clear separation of religion and education under the new government.

No prejudice will be allowed to anyone seeking an education. It will be law.

Home schooling will not be necessary with this new education program but can be an option if it meets the stringent guidelines established.

This new focus will be to encourage and enforce the law that all Americans complete their required education without distractions and needless interruptions. *The American Republic* educational system will be of the finest in the world.

The first 21 years of a person's life will be with family and education. That will be followed by 3 years of military service, completion of advance education if desired, and then professional career and life.

By age 25, a person should be of mature character and experience, closely influenced by a good government with strong family values. Those who wish to change their career, no matter how seemingly insignificant, will also be allowed to re-educate themselves at no cost to them.

Retirement will be based on each individual's choice to participate in the success of the business in which they are employed.

Absolutely no prejudice will be tolerated against any American who wishes to better themselves and contribute to the continued success of the Homeland. Philosophus Autodidactus. Ḥayy ibn Yaqẓān.

X.   Health and Welfare

The health of a nation is not measured by profits and losses. America is not just protected by a good system of government, it needs a system of health that protects the entire population against any disease or affliction that seeks to infect any citizen of its population.

This requires introducing a preventative health system that will insure that everyone has the best care afforded, without prejudice.

What is good for the leader of America is also good for all people of America. This same care will be afforded to every American citizen. There will be no out of pocket expense of any kind; there will be no more private hospitals and staff taking advantage of the sick and the healthy; and there will be no more private businesses that are in charge of the medications and equipment needed to keep America healthy.

Nationalizing the entire healthcare industry is the only way to guarantee that every American will be taken care of from birth to death, without the worry of expense for good care.

The government of *The American Republic* will guarantee to the American people that any disease that is left without a cure will be number one on the list for research funding.   Cures will never be kept from those who need them. Any business, research facility, or hospital staff that keeps medications, treatments, and therapies from the American people that cause suffering and death will be brought before Congress and punished by death under law. Anyone who willfully withholds this type of information or does not sincerely seek out cures and treatments are guilty of murder or attempted murder of American citizens,.

A strong nation is a healthy one. People who are free from the burdens of sickness and disease are happier citizens.

Social programs will be such that any family member suffering from dysfunction will be provided for until they are cured. If a cure is not deemed feasible, then that citizen will be cared for with dignity and respect until their death.

Facilities will be of the highest quality for the sick. They will be of the same caliber as would be for a leader of a nation.

There will be no need for welfare funds, for all-able bodied Americans will be either in school, the military, business, or government service. Those who are severely disabled will be provided for in a facility that will accommodate their every need.

A strong nation has tough, healthy, educated citizens. By providing and supporting health and social programs to keep Americans in good physical and mental health, all will eventually be better in America. Citizens will have no more worry about out of pocket funds for any medical or social welfare problem.

Drugs that are not conducive to the human body will be eliminated. Homeopathic medicine will be employed as much as possible if found to positively treat sickness and disease and maintain the health of others.

Medical practice will be of a high order. There will be no more private

practice. Medical practitioners will receive ongoing training to provide the

best of the best in medicine. All will adhere to the Hippocratic Oath. Any

deviations from the rule of law will be severely punished.

Senior citizens or any disabled person will never go without well-trained

medical care professionals. Their needs will be met without compromise.

This also includes all mental health and social family disorders.

The appropriate well-trained practitioner will be assigned a reasonable

caseload. Care facilities will be designed in resort style to provide the

sincere comfort needed by a person for recovery or hospice.

XI. National Security

The security of a nation in this age is vitally important for the survival of its people.

With eclectic weapons systems and clandestine operations that infest nations, it is of the highest priority to keep America safe from all traitors and outside infiltrators.

It is important to have an intelligence center that gathers, distributes, responds, reacts, engages, and resolves. This center of knowledge is the core to keeping America safe. This is why a national database will be kept on everything that is American: its people, places, and things. This is why law will require a national Identification System. As mentioned before, these Nano chips will be implanted into every citizen of *The American Republic*. The National registry will have data on virtually everything that is known on that person. The implant will be the only way to track a person's location, purchase transactions, selling transactions, and interactions with daily activities relative to life. If civil liberties come into question it would be a valid argument. However, with the current crime rate, immigration issues, covert espionage and other transactions that now go unnoticed, a system of control like this must and will be installed. With this type of system, it will be difficult for a child or adult to become lost or kidnapped; crimes against humanity will no longer go without being on record.

Illegal immigration will be completely controlled by this system, for without an implant, no one will be able to enter or leave America undetected.

It is vital and important to keep America safe, not just from outside sources, but also from within. There are many who have the propensity to do crime. The streets of our Nation are not in control by the local law enforcement or our government.

It is not a question of what is right for some, but what is right for all. America has one of the highest crime rates of all nations, and *The American Republic* will not tolerate this. Having weapons in a nation of violent people is not the answer; in fact, it leads to eventual violence. Strict gun control will never be the answer, because weapons will always find a way in. With a safe nation, one will not need weapons to defend their person, family, or home.

A secure nation is one that protects the safety of its citizens at all costs. America must be under control and discipline until this failing system of government has been completely eradicated.

International organizations and foreign governments just cannot keep their preying eyes and ears from gathering data and influencing American government to their benefit. These international organizations and foreign governments that have infiltrated our commerce and government will be ferreted out, and if found guilty of irreparable harm against America, those responsible will be hunted down and severely punished under law. Because of our current open border policies and antiquated border protection systems protocols, "aliens" from distant lands continue to invade us. Open borders use to be a good idea. The borders will be protected against intruders who have no legal right to be in America. We have become a nation that has allowed other nations to infect our society with false propaganda, and other covert operations. It is important for the very survival of America to unearth all agencies and independent contractors that are counterproductive to the policies of *The American Republic*. These infestations will be caught and exported back to their countries of origin, or put to a tribunal where if found guilty, severely punished under law.

The American Republic will review any functional National Security agency existing under the current rule of government. It will evaluate the agencies for need. The successful clandestine and covert operations that keep our nation safe from those that wish to destroy America will continue. *The American Republic* will have organizations sanctioned by Congress to carry out National Security operations with no compromise to funds or jurisdiction. This will insure the sovereignty of our nation, and protect without prejudice, the citizens of the *American Republic*.

Many centuries have gone by in America with no true balance of freedom, peace, and governance. Corruption seems to be the norm. Americans have become apathetic to the world around them. Propaganda has become a tool used to deploy this apathy to the masses. Americans have become lost, and must be found and redirected back into the American dream. This roundup will not be easy, thus a few more restraints on civil liberties. Americans either fear or mistrust their government and its law enforcement. A new trusting government will be the Mother and Father of the Homeland that will be dedicated to protecting and serving its citizens, completely.

It is difficult but not impossible to manage a people, as long as those people have the faith and trust in those placed in the stewardship of a nation.

There will be one police force that will directly report to a department within the National Security of *The American Republic*. No more Federal agencies of law. No more civic police controlled by state or local government. No more corrupt law enforcement. No more, fear for The People of America.

Congress will define new responsibilities and accountabilities, and a strong well-equipped force will be the primary goal. Unfortunately, complete control of a nation is the only way to guarantee true civil liberties. Extraterrestrials are as an integral part of our National Security as they are with other nations. As stated above, it remains in the best interests of the American people to let the speculations of their existence continue. *The*

American Republic will continue to welcome and respect their continuance

on our soil. Until we have complete control over the destinies of

Americans, the extraterrestrial phenomenon will still be as evasive as God.

XII.   Trail of Tears, Indigenous Peoples of the Americas

It is unfortunate that the original founders of America were not true to their word with this land's original inhabitants. *The American Republic* recognizes that tribal peoples have been shuffled under the rug of history since the landing of America's first settlers. Their lands were stolen from them by lies, coercion, and force of arms by those not even worthy of living in America. In most cases, these natural citizens were hoodwinked for centuries by the American government leadership, only to be paid off with worthless trinkets, and lastly, government wastelands.

The American Republic will not tolerate governments existing within governments in America any longer. It is in the best interest of a people to never lose sight of their heritage and culture, and will never conflict with the system of government and laws.

The American Republic will not recognize American government treaties and other inducements drafted specifically for the tribes of people inhabiting this Nation. Those agreements and covenants granted by a corrupt system of government will not be incorporated into the new government of America. However, what will be honored under the new government will be restitutions due to those decedents of the American tribes of the original inhabitants. The current American government is responsible for the crimes committed against theses tribes and treaties or contracts breached. All such pacts will be evaluated before being acted upon, and must garner the consent of both Congress and the various tribal clans still existing in America. In an effort to earn forgiveness from these tribal people, Congress will be given the charge to explore every feasible and equitable form of restitution.

All reservations that have been legally confining and segregating the tribal peoples of America will be disbanded and no longer exist under law.

Tribal peoples will be encouraged to set up in communities so they can be fruitful and multiply under nature's laws. We are all citizens of America. Gambling will not be the primary source of income for the tribal people; in fact, gambling will be highly regulated under new law, and only permitted to operate within 30 miles of incorporated communities.

The same laws and benefits that apply to Americans will also apply to all tribal peoples.

They were the first Americans of this Nation and thus have long earned their rights and privileges to enjoy life here. A formal apology will be given to the tribal people of America for who have suffered so long. Restitutions cannot even begin to satisfy the suffering and humiliation that these tribal peoples have endured at the hands of the American government.

Tribal peoples will be recognized as the Americans of America without any stain from the past. Their great history will become part of the culture of America, and will be taught in all schools of learning. Their culture will become an integral part of American history without any compromise of the truth.

XIII.   Extraterrestrials, Puma Punku

Humans are a result of careful planning by nature's laws with the specific selection and manipulation of genes. This has led to the human race that exists today. However, long before humans were created by nature on planet earth, beings from other universes have been visiting, living, and dying on our planet.

For millions of years humans have been witness to so many wonders of nature. The universe has brought to us so many seeds of life. These extraterrestrial beings have been earth's guardians for many centuries, and will continue watching over us long after we have left earth's terra to explore what is beyond.

The military and other "dark" groups have been very careful in the dissemination of the existence of extraterrestrials to the public. There are prominent technologies in use today that have been gleaned from encounters with beings from other worlds. Their knowledge has been passed through generations of earth's inhabitants in the form of words, symbols, monuments, religions, and hardware. Only a select few are ever determined to be recipients of this enlightenment. Through the ages, it has only been this small handful of humans they have entrusted with the truths and knowledge they wish us to possess.

All of us have been given choices, by those who have been made privy to these truths. Even though these choices were eclectic, in most cases humans still failed to make prudent judgments. It has been these culminations of so many unwise decisions, when set against the truths that have led these beings to keep their existence hidden from the general masses. These life forms have for so long affected and shaped the workings of this planet, that their influences have been taken for granted. Arrogant humans now presume to have invented, created, and discovered all that exists, on their own. Despite this, extraterrestrials will continue to assist humans in order to advance the planet. However, as long as we continue supporting bad government, bad religion, and bad ecological conservation of earth's natural resources, they will maintain anonymity and the truth will never be revealed to all.

America or any other Nation on planet earth will not be prepared for the truth of extraterrestrials, until its people have changed. Until then, the current system of government will continue playing cat and mouse with the public as to whether they exist, or not.

This truth will definitely set all humans free.

XIV. Nationalization

The American Republic is not just an idea, but also a purpose, that has been aided and nurtured by the very ones who have been its faithful citizens. It has become our duty and obligation to protect what we know until Americans and the rest of earth's populous have become one with themselves and their respective governments.

America has lost its unique position as a paradigm in the world of business, and has descended to no more than a social carrier of economic disease. This fiscal disorder has mutated into a fractal of businesses that have robbed too many, rewarded even less, and left the destitute the remaining majority. False promises coupled with sacrificing all to grab hold of the almighty dollar have completely torn apart the very fabric of the American Dream.

Our government promised this phantom dream to us. This covenant guaranteed its citizens inalienable freedoms of reward, and prosperity. The individual citizen, their family, and their communities were to benefit from it all. It has collapsed.

America needs a system to produce ideas and solutions to pressing social, economic, ecological, and scientific issues. All Americans will be encouraged to provide for the common good of their fellow citizens, and for the common defense of their nation. All Americans, not just some, will reap the benefits of America's successes. *The American Republic* will have no class system, no poor, no rich, and no illiterate or uneducated citizens. Every American will exist at the top of the "economic chain." The new government of *The American Republic* will have its Congress define all resources and private businesses that are in the interests of The People of America. Once The People and their Congress agree upon these resources, those selected entities will become property of *The American Republic* government under the Nationalization program. The citizens employed by these entities will be evaluated for service value, placed, and will begin working for their new government employer. The merit of upper echelon management will also be assessed, and any managers with valuable skills will remain employed by the new government. Those not surviving the cut will be re-educated and compensated with wages decided upon by Congress. All outside business interests will be frozen and re-evaluated under new rules of law, and any business entities residing within the borders of America not wishing to comply will be asked to leave America, leaving all assets in the control of the new government of America. We wish them the best.

In order to gain full control of our nation's assets, business interests and resources, we will nationalize and control every sector of the business arena as it relates to this nation's and its people's interests. *The American Republic* will fully realize in advance that these seizures will create panic within America as well as without, but there must be a complete accounting and control of all attributes. Imports and exports will be under absolute jurisdiction of *The American Republic*. Transportation and any other direct or indirect link to products or services will be under control of the new government. Government subsidized public and private businesses have all but destroyed America. Those entities guilty of prostituting their workforces to other nations will be barred from doing business in America. This practice will be unacceptable under *The American Republic*, while funding will no longer be made available to them.

This Nation will once again manufacture what its citizens need; we will regain our "Made in America" status.

Congress and The People will be the ones to fashion the new rule of law for America's nationalization policies. Viable employment for Americans is primary. Those who have been shamed into retirement or who still believe they can contribute to the overall American workforce, will be welcomed.

Nationalization will be the only way forward for America to gain its independence from self-serving business interests. The rape and pillage of American ingenuity and talent has gone on long enough. There exists zero tolerance in *The American Republic* for those who wish to sell off our nation's assets to the highest foreign bidders, and most despicably, to those who will stoop to sell out our citizens. Nationalization is a matter of National Security for the safety and survival of our great nation! Nationalization of telecommunications, fuels, transportation, electricity, education, health and welfare and any other resource or service deemed important for the benefit of the citizens of *The American Republic* will be placed under government control. We can do what we teach.

XV. Hate Groups

From the time humankind first organized into groups for survival, there has existed a dislike for many of the basic physical differences. Humans should have logically evolved in such a way to have suppressed these sophomoric emotions of dislike, hate, prejudice, or anger.

Somewhere within history, humans lost the initial gift of discernment and have allowed on their emotions to dictate to them their behavior in relating to other humans.

Prejudice, ignorance, religion, commerce, politics and the choice to hate another without justifiable reason, has led to the obliteration of millions of people throughout humankind's history. The laws then, and those enacted most recently have only functioned as a temporary deterrent to those who overtly and surreptitiously hate.

The American Republic recognizes these faults in humans, but will never tolerate hate in any form against another. Laws will be enacted to discourage those from carrying out this selective genocide in America. Although it will be nearly impossible to completely eradicate hate and prejudice from the minds of humans, *The American Republic* will require firmer control through new laws and more severe punishment.

A temporary solution to repopulate the tribal reservation wastelands within America with those who cannot eradicate the hating of others from their character will be a possible solution. Racial or gender prejudice will no longer be allowed to flourish amongst the citizens and will be kept under strict supervision for rehabilitation by a specific department of *The American Republic*.

Isolation of these people or groups into controlled reservations will be the only way to expose deviant citizens. They will not form a government within a government. As American citizens, they will still answer to the laws of the land. No person or group residing in any rehabilitation reservation will usurp the laws of *The American Republic*. This will be punishable under law.

The expense of relocation will not be an issue, for the resources can be spared for the needs of the majority.

Exposure to and suffering through hate is not healthy for the American character, especially when the time for new government is at hand. Having these identified deviant's isolated from cooperative citizens, housed in recognized locations throughout America will undoubtedly work to deter others from the like. It is best to know where the hate is rather than having it living next door. It is vital for the continued success of a nation to have people working together for a common good.

Anything else is counterproductive and will lead to continued chaos. There is no place in America for hatred and prejudice.

XVI. Money

There are no laws known to nature that can account for the use of what humans call money. There are, however, human-made laws based on exchange for products or services.

The mechanics of money have evolved over the centuries into a very complicated ball of twine. To discuss this intricate process would only lead to a tenuous heap of pages and ideas.

Many alternative methods of exchange have yet to be explored.

For some reasons only known to humans, there exists a perverse attraction to shiny things. This curiosity has seemed to have lead to our modern day addiction to the gathering and spending of money. So much pain, suffering, and loss of life have been the result of humans and their self-imposed relationship with money.

So many words to describe this ancient co-dependency, fiat system, fractional reserve, debt, interest, resource based, credit money, and many other words to confuse the unaware.

A complete inventory of America's resources is crucial. An unconditional accounting of its systems as they relate to banking will be thoroughly analyzed.

A central bank of *The American Republic* will be the only way to fully control a money-based system.

Congress with the help of The People will explore other ways of exchange for goods or services that would be in the best interest of Americans.

The elimination of all debt to all Americans will be the first start to our nation's fiscal recovery.

The complete balancing of any budget will be effortless, once all debts have been cleared.

Any internal revenue system that controls the taxes and other incomes will be re-organized to benefit, not burden The People.

Basing an economic system on scarcity, abundance, or both, will be evaluated.

The undue suffering of Americans because of the scarcity of money will be no more.

The abundance of a method of exchange for all Americans will be the primary goal of the government of *The American Republic*.

No more self-serving reserve banks operating independently of government will exist.

Emergence of thought will be the only way that a nation will be able to come out of this money addiction. *The American Republic* will spread the wealth of a nation based on deeds and legitimate service.

Money, if not properly managed, is the root of despair for some and the glory of wealth for others. Americans cannot and will not be consumed by the pangs of poverty.

Human's addiction to the need for money has evolved into a disease and curse to humans. This dependence must be purged and a more relevant means of exchange developed if humans are to live for a better America and a better world.

XVII.   Conflict

War is yet another word to describe differences between people.

Governments and businesses today operate as facades. Operating under color of law, they utilize deceptive operations to fool those ignorant to the charade.

So many lives are lost because of conflict.

The new government of *The American Republic* will not engage in any unnecessary theaters of conflict. If no other nation directly or indirectly threatens America or its citizens, then we will leave them alone. However, if they are found to be in violation of our Rights as Humans, we will eviscerate their lands and their people, without mercy.

If needed, we will negotiate with other nations for shared resources. We will not take by force for selfish reasons. We will not exploit the weak. We will temper our anger and find ways to accommodate those who are slow in understanding. War breeds war. War is the lowest form of excuse that any human can come up with to justify a means to an end. However, if one has lost all reason and diplomacy, then war is just.

Moreover, with it comes complete destruction of the opponent without mercy.

The current system of the United Nations is a mockery to diplomacy. Its current armed forces are also a travesty to the age-old military philosophy. All treaties with so-called allied nations are in contempt of the peace and stability within the so-called "free world."

There is no "free world," there is only a world of conflict.

America is only as powerful as The People thinks it is. Without that conviction, America is no different from any other and is subject to the same fate of any other self-boasting nation in power. It is true that America has technological abilities when it comes to military posturing, but many other nations stand equal in that position. Many more are slowly making their way into that arena and cannot be ignored.

Under new government leadership, *The American Republic* will distance itself from those wishing to exploit the weak and innocent. It will however defend those having legitimate grievances effecting the population at large. Ultimately, a "One World" system of government will be the end solution to the numerous, senseless conflicts that distract millions from the planet's goal of freedom and prosperity.

Peace is the only absolute solution to war, and will be the primary goal for *The American Republic* government to achieve.

First, *The American Republic* will get Americas "house" in order before looking into the "houses" of others.

Any of America's conflicts with other nations or any conflicts existing between other nations that are not rightfully justified will not be supported. *The American Republic* recognizes that religious differences are not an excuse for war. Humans have been afforded the natural right and privilege of choice, and will not have that taken away.

XVIII.   American Society

Every American has the right to be free and live in a society that protects them without fear.

The true family unit has become almost extinct because of this fear.

People are afraid to go outside because of the uncertainty in their lives.

Americans have lost the innocence of community. Why can't we leave our doors unlocked at night? Why can't we trust our neighbor? Why can't we have faith that our government will protect us in our homes?

Fear and panic are ruining the streets of America. Violence and crime have become the norm in this Nation because police have become a self-serving and corrupt department of city, state, and federal government. Households have become broken, because the failing economy has forced both parents to be employed. Schools are raising America's children because of absent parents. City streets are raising America's children because of absent parents. Degenerate citizens are now impressing America's children because absent parents have no ability to influence. America's children have become video game playing, mp3 listening, and cell phone texting digital nomads within their own family and community. America's children must be paid more attention to or our Nation will not progress. These are our future leaders, educators, trades people, and parents. How can we entrust with them, our America, when they cannot decipher a common mathematical problem, write a complete paragraph, or

---

comprehend a basic novel.

This government has abandoned both our children and our adults and this must be remedied.

American society has lost focus of its origin.

The basic principles established so long ago by those governing our people left out too many of its citizens in the design. As mentioned, those same people who helped form a perfect union, themselves forgot about the indigenous masses sharing the very same land and the inclusion of women in the initial philosophical design of the Nation. This will be corrected.

Americans, wishing for more freedoms, broke away from the colonies ruled then by Britannia. Tired of the trickery and lies, these settlers decided amongst themselves to separate from the tyrannical rule of the colonial empire ruled by a bad King. With the help from other nations, this new idea for independence began to take form.

The rest is history. You, the reader, can research the voluminous Manifestum of ideas that have been written about the original American Dream.

The American Republic will guarantee to each citizen a perfect form of government, with rights and privileges decided by Congress and The People. Americans deserve the best of the best in government with support. *Made in America* will be a primary objective. Citizens will not fear corporate or government retaliation for offering ideas to improve our nation's commerce and leadership. Rewards will be great for those with vision. There will be massive programs to rebuild America to greatness. With a strong support system of government, dreams can and will become reality. America was built on these dreams, and so it shall be, again. We will wipe the tarnish from our "stars" so they shine once again. We will find our "eagle" and nurture it back to health and strength. Our "eagle" will fly high over every mountain on planet earth spreading the Good News! Prejudices will not be tolerated. We will resolve our differences and become a nation of strong free people. Respect and honor will be given to those reaching the age of legitimate retirement, because these people have assured our places in the future America.

XIX.   Prisons and Punishments

From the inception of humanity, humans have been committing crimes against humans. Humans have over the centuries tried to define laws to protect fellow inhabitants, but it has been without much success. Punishment has not been serving as an effective deterrent, and the incarcerated are not being suitably rehabilitated to re-enter society as productive citizens.

America's prisons are being stocked with many people who should not even be in the system. A sentence should be commensurate with the crime. Privatization of the prison system is not the answer to renovating the penal institution. In *The American Republic*, prisons will become part of the government nationalization program, and will be managed by those who truly understand punishment and rehabilitation. The prison systems will no longer be controlled by local, state, and private entities. A department within *The American Republic* will be designated to manage and have full control of America's penal institutions.

Again, we could go on through volumes of data debating about the rights and privileges of the incarcerated. Human rights groups will still have a voice in this new proposed system of prisoner rehabilitation and punishment.

The entire system of law and punishment will have to be re-evaluated as it relates to specific levels of crimes. There are far too many people incarcerated for minor drug offences, mental illness, and for crimes that have not intentionally injured or taken a life. Prisons will be for those who have taken life without just cause, raped, intentionally caused irreversible pain, suffering, or death of a citizen, committed treason and other yet defined heinous crimes. These are the crimes whose perpetrators should suffer the severest of penalties. Death will be the solution for those criminals. This decree will include even those prisoners currently in the American penal systems whose crimes against humans qualify for this ultimate punishment.

This means that all who have been convicted of identified crimes will be evaluated by a team of reviewers from within a department of *The American Republic*. If the team's decision finds them guilty, the offending individual will be severely punished under law within 3 days of final judgment. This course of action may seem cruel and unjust under current law, but we can add a twist to an inmate's fate: Members of a victim's family can be added to the team of reviewers to decide that criminal's fate. There will exist a diverse means of how death sentences will be administered to an inmate found guilty of a heinous crime: Death by hanging; lethal injection; electrocution; decapitation; burned at the stake; boiled alive; fed to wild beasts or insects, given deadly viruses or doses of lethal radiation, and execution by firing squad with a weapon of the executioner's choice. Employing the use of prisoners for scientific experimentations instead of innocent animals will also be visited.

Those inmates left behind because their crimes did not reach the level to be labeled heinous will undergo complete reform. No lagging in cells 24 hours a day. Education and skills training will be their punishment until it has been determined by a rehabilitation team that they have become completely reformed.

Those found worthy of this new program will become part of the immense workforce required to rebuild America. Strict rules and a watchful electronic eye will keep order, because idle minds with no direction are a brew for trouble. Congress and committee for this bold new program for placing prisoners in a national education and workforce program will have the task to work out the specific mechanics.

The entire prison system will be overhauled to ensure that inmates, who were never guilty of the crimes they were convicted of, will be reviewed and freed. Those who are truly guilty will be reviewed for their level of crime and selected for death, or the national prison program for education and work.

XX. Transportation

Oil has been the excuse for so many problems, crimes, wars, treason, and civil unrest on planet earth. We have designed our technology around it without considerations to the environment and to those living in it.

We humans have become very mobile over the centuries. With this mobility has come great concern with the way our transportation has evolved. Have the designers and planners really been looking for ways to ensure that the ease in transportation is met? Changes to policies are influenced by politics and business. America's forward thinking process has been purposefully stalled.

Our mass transportation system is antiquated by design. The automotive industry prefers to sell inefficient vehicles that consume way too much natural resources. The oil industry is in concert with that industry to insure its financial agenda. There is no environmental incentive to produce fuel-efficient vehicles, only monetary incentive not to. In addition, that financial pressure of the few far outweighs the needs of the many.

Until America is brought back from its current descent, all transportation in America will come under direct control of *The American Republic*. Nationalizing this industry is necessary to guarantee technologic excellence and environmental safeguards.

The air, rail, and ground transportation industries falls within this category. It is vitally important that extreme control of these types of industries be in effect until America has conquered its transportation woes.

XXI. American Retirees

Americans have long been engaged in contributing to their community, with no sincere recognition from the government. Those who are recognized are rare. Every American is a contributor to the success of this Nation, and when their time comes for retirement, they must and will be cared for.

Those who have saved additional funds, as well as, those who have not will be treated equally with *The American Republic* Retirement Program. This program will guarantee that each individual has the best of the best in care. Whether they are of the able body, or convalescent, or have suffered some dis-ease with their health, this will never be an issue. They will also have a retirement fund that will be theirs when they need it for whatever reason, all managed and controlled by a department in *The American Republic* government.

All who have reached the age or choice to retire can and will do so in the luxury of kings.

America's current system of care for its seniors is barbaric. We will not cast our precious jewels into the dust for others to trample over and forget. When people see a senior citizen, they will find it natural to give that person the respect due. These learned souls have worked hard during their lifetimes to assure us our future, and we owe them that. Most Americans have forsaken their elders, placing them in lonely holding cells masquerading as retirement facilities, awaiting death. Americans have all but forgotten that without the perseverance of those who experienced the past, America would not exist as any form of a nation today.

The American Republic with Congress will pass laws and enforce laws to protect all those Americans who have retired, and wish to live a life of peace and tranquility. As precarious as America is now, we still must and will care for our sick and helpless. These citizens will not live in isolation anymore, they will not be without adequate finance, food, and housing, and they will be recognized and respected. These are our parents; these are our citizens.

XXII. Animal and Insect Guarantees

Animals and insects are part of nature's ballet of life on planet earth. We humans have a tendency to destroy what we believe to be inferior or incidental. We have encroached on the lands of the animals and insects. Humans have designed technology that has disrupted nature's balance. Humans use animals and insects for pleasure, sport, and experimentation. Even though humans have evolved, they still fail to consider the consequences of their actions against the very creatures that were left in their care.

Over farming of animals for profit is another horrendous problem befalling animals. *The American Republic* will heavily regulate and enforce such practices to bring this industry under control for the health and benefit of the animals farmed and consumed by Americans.

Experimentation on any animal is criminal. Humans now have the tools and the intellect to use other means to discover cures. Advanced scientific computer technology can be utilized to simulate nearly every ailment and calculate remedies and sources for remedies.

Law will forbid any animal experimentation for any reason. America's animal rights activists have made some headway in securing minor laws to protect against this savage display of animal cruelty. Any person found guilty of cruelty to domestic and wild animals will face a punishment of either death, or incarceration depending upon the degree of the offense.

The same will apply to those found guilty of wantonly destroying insects needed to balance nature's ecosystem. Insects that cannot coexist with our farmed crops will be deterred. Insects can and will be used to improve farming, and there are natural insect repellants that will be explored for use as a replacement for harmful insecticides. In our wisdom, we will find ways to accommodate insects and use them to improve our environment, lifestyle, and our food chain.

The human body was not designed to live off the flesh of animals. Human's teeth, jaws, and digestive system support a fleshless diet. Our front teeth are not sharp for tearing meats, our molars are for grinding vegetation, and our lengthy digestive system does not easily breakdown consumed flesh. Humans tend to make it a choice to consume the flesh of beasts along with supplemental plant materials to get adequate nutrients. It has been the invention of refrigeration and other technologies that has made the consumption of meats more accessible to humans.

It is understood that in most cultures, the art of consuming flesh is practiced, and in some areas, that is the only food source. In America, we do not need to depend on flesh to keep our bodies strong. Humans have developed technologies that can give us great-tasting, nutritional food sources to lessen our reliance on flesh as a primary food source. Choosing to eat or not eat the flesh of animals will be a hard choice to make, and cannot yet be mandated by a government, but it should be considered if citizens want to live longer and healthier lives.

As caretakers of planet earth, one must consider all options when it comes to feeding a population. Our intellect gives us the tools which can make all things possible.

Animals and insects each have inherent rights to live as nature intended, alongside humans without humankind's thirst for their destruction.

All animal sports will be banned. These practices are cruel, and it is brutal to breed and raise an animal for a life of combat and racing. Animals fulfill a need when they are used to assist in farming, law enforcement, rehabilitation and travel. Animals were never intended to satisfy human gratification.

Animal sanctuaries can and will be established and maintained for animals and insects that have been rescued from natural disasters in the environment, or from poachers. No longer will zoos exist as concrete and metal "prisons" for wildlife. A department in the government will regulate all sanctuaries and animal wildlife habitats so that they mirror the animal's natural lifestyle.

Fishing is also a business that will be heavily regulated. The senseless slaughter of whales, dolphins and other mammals will be eliminated and enforced under law. Anyone caught killing, capturing, spearing, or netting these and other creatures of the sea and land will face death, or severe punishment. International treaties are but words on paper with no real intent to carry out or uphold the rules that were agreed upon. If any animal law is broken on any body of water, air space, or land falling within the jurisdiction of *The American Republic*, will also suffer the same fate if caught and properly tried in a court of law.

Under *The American Republic*, organizations that attempt to protect the animal kingdom will no longer be necessary. The department formed will directly oversee this immense issue, and all businesses and cultures that have historically been intertwined with various creatures of planet earth will be investigated for merit.

Americans will learn to live more cohesively with the animals and insects that inhabit the lands of America and the rest of our planet. There is no excuse for animal or insect abuse. *The American Republic* will not tolerate any abuse to any animal or insect. Pet caretakers come with same set of rules and punishments. It would be prudent to educate young minds of the fair treatment to be bestowed upon any domesticated animal living as a citizen's pet. We must ask ourselves what is best for the pet. Pet caretaking is a privilege not a right. If a citizen's heart and soul is into true companionship, then having that creature under your care will be the pet caretaker's responsibility and accountability. Animal hospitals and clinics will be established and managed by the same animal rights and regulations department of the America Republic. All domesticated animals designated as pets will be registered and inoculated against diseases. There will be no rampant over-breeding of pets, and no puppy mills. Their still needs to be discussion and debate on whether an animal should be spay or neutered. Caretakers will be held responsible for their pets. Animals will not be running free in parks, beaches, streets, or unfenced yards. If an animal is caught loose without proper registration, the caretaker will be fined on a progressive scale, and given seven days to bring the animal up to code or face incarceration. Housing of any animal under the animal and insect program of *The American Republic* will never be put to death unless for medical reason. They will be found a place to live out their lives. There will be no more excuses for the lack of care of domestic animals living in America. Domesticated, sanctuary and wildlife habitat animals will fall under the same government sponsored health and welfare programs as their caretakers. All animals will have access to the same medical care as humans. The protection of the creature kingdom will not only be protected under enforceable law, but will become an eventual way of life in America. Zoo's for pleasure, circus businesses, and any other display of animals for pleasure will be outlawed and eliminated.

Nature has allowed humans to evolve to the level of caretaker of planet earth. We will not disappoint those who have allowed us all to flourish on this planet.

XXIII.   Taxes

Taxes are a way of financial control over the masses. The forceful collection of a tax for goods or services is not the right way for a Nation to insure financial stability for its people.

In order to have a strong nation, you need strong people, not taxed people. The new government of *The American Republic* will eliminate the current tax system, and impose a new and equitable system of taxation on its citizens.

A tax system should be used to manage and improve the nation's infrastructure, technology, armed services, resource allocation, and any other service that is required to help improve the lives of all of its citizens without prejudice.

If a system of tax is well managed then there is no need to continually raise taxes. One of many reasons for our soaring taxes in America, today, is the lack of prudent spending coupled with a gross mismanagement of funds.

A voluntary tax would be acceptable. All citizens will share a common goal for America. Congress with ideas from The People will impose a tax system that is reasonable to all.

A national tax is a good start; the percentage should be decided by Congress influenced by The People from their districts. Taxes on domestic goods will need to be decided upon by The People and Congress.

The goal is not to have taxes and other outside expenses become a burden on any American.

Americans must and will live a good life free from the burdens of high taxes and other financial burdens. Everyone will contribute. Exemptions will not be necessary under this new tax plan.

The import and export taxes between states and other nations will have to be overhauled to assist in the elimination of the burdens on any nation's gross national product.

Nationalization of America's major resources, goods, and services will guarantee that a balanced budget will be accomplished.

It is quite apparent that the current state of the union in America is in a deep economic depression. It is unfortunate that so many Americans have been left floundering in debt because of the current government's greed and the allowance of business banks, lobbyists and other carpetbaggers to influence the current and past administrations. The American government has allowed so many business interests to circumvent The Uniform Commercial Code that it has severely weakened our financial stability. America has been up to its eyebrows in debt for longer than they would like to admit, and there is no relief in sight. This government has been covering the losses from their financial recklessness by taxing us, their citizens.

This government has displayed no regard for the lives of its own citizens with this brazen practice. Our elected public servants have flimflammed us all by allowing our economic system to be destroyed alongside the lives of millions of Americans.

There is no true sense of direction for Americans. They have become entangled in economic debt and other slave-to- master relationships. It is time for Americans to change their way of government to insure that the burden of unfair taxation is no longer on the backs of its citizens.

A well-planned economy with strong leadership will be the only way to insure stability in America. Plans must be made to use homegrown intellect and ingenuity to overcome the money pit that keeps Americans chained to their paychecks. There are many people in America with ideas on improving the financial position of America. They just need a chance to be heard.

The American Republic will not allow Americans to be burdened anymore with excessive taxes.

There is plenty of work that needs to done to rebuild America, our Home, into the dream that we all share.

XXIV. Employment

In America, there are millions of geniuses just waiting for a chance to demonstrate their skills or knowledge of a trade. Every trade has value, without exception.

It is exceedingly important that every American be prepared to participate in the rebuilding of America's infrastructure, which includes more than just its bridges, rails, and highways. It means houses, buildings, communities, cities and all of the inner workings that are needed to make this Nation a viable and safe place to live for families, retirees, and citizens.

We do not intend to interfere with the social interactions between people, but what we can do as a new government is create an environment that is conducive for those social interactions to take place, undisturbed by social criticism.

The American Republic Government will bring back all trades to America, without exception. *The American Republic* will make sure that Americans are first on the employment lists. Any business that exports its human resources offshore will be considered un-American and disallowed. If that business insists on exclusive offshore employment, then *The American Republic* government will revoke their license (Charter) to do business in America. America will not do business with those companies that do not think *American* first.

"Made in America" will come back with quality and care, as was in the past. There will be no need for private unions, a department within government will provide the same benefits and safe working conditions for working citizens than any private union can. The trade unions will be under government control. This organized crime business will be no more. *The American Republic* is offering a system that guarantees every American employment, either through private enterprise or through the government. It is the duty of America government, to provide opportunities for its citizens to earn a proper living.

Even a lemonade stand that offers the weary traveler refreshment is a business.

It is highly unlikely that any American will be out of work under the new system of government because of well thought out planned checks and balances to insure the success of the new trade programs. Jobs exported off shore will be brought back to America. Once every American is enjoying some sort of earned income, then offshore commerce can be considered. *The American Republic* recognizes that global business is the future, but understands that providing for our family at home comes before providing for others. With that comes the strength and will to help others.

XXV. Law

Law is another word denoting a system of interpretative rules that control the lives of humans. Humans have had laws for centuries, with not much success.

Under the current system of law, a nation must have an army in order to enforce its laws, without it, people will do, as they will. It is highly unlikely that America or any other nation will be able to have laws free from force.

Unfortunately not everyone can be pleased with every law, thus a system must be designed to insure some sense of value for the nation. There are many systems of law that govern every aspect of a person's life, all of which will be abolished or re-written for the benefit of Americans.

A supreme court is yet another layer that again symbolizes some superior system of judgment to direct the destinies of all who are forced to accept its judgment of rulings.

Courts resolve disputes and determine the fates of those who **do not** follow the law.

The entire court system in America will be re-engineered to benefit the citizens who are truly innocent. The current judicial system is imperfect and corrupt, and will be reconstituted.

Having a title of judge is an honor and thus must be given only to those who are truly as knowledgeable in the law as they are just in their decisions. There will never be just one judge in any court, a panel of people who are wise will always oversee and determine rulings. Religion cannot become part of the law of America. God has no place in human law. Thus, no religious books of any kind will be used in a court of law as a tool to terrorize citizens into speaking the truth. There are no guarantees that one will tell the truth, thus the facts must be made clear. It is not the fear of GOD that should make a citizen reveal the truth, but the fear of the consequences for speaking falsehoods that should cause them pause.

XXVI.   Freedom of Speech and of the Press

Every human on planet earth has the right to speak and write as they feel without the fear of punishment or death. Publishing the truth will be praised. However, the publishing of untruths that adversely affect another will be punished under law.

Libel and slander will be punished under law, if the defamations and/or accusations are not found to be true. Opinions are just that, opinions. However, speaking threats of bodily harm against another or another's family will be noted, especially if violent intent can be determined.

The government of *The American Republic* will guarantee freedom of speech and of the press to every American as long as they follow the simple guidelines established by The People and Congress. Merely expressing a belief in something that does not adversely affect America or its citizens cannot be actionable on its face. However, if it is discovered that this belief is a scheme for something more sinister that will affect *The American Republic* or its citizens, then its proponent will be investigated.

A sane person is quite capable of making the choice to tell the truth, and most humans are inherently good and do not want to be deceitful. We all make right and wrong choices, and what we do with these choices becomes our destiny.

It is not that difficult to determine and understand this simple concept of free speech and of the press.

For centuries, humans have been prejudiced by their egos. As a result, they try to discourage those wishing to express opinion. For centuries, this suppression of spoken and written word has been successfully accomplished through fear, death, or shame. If citizens feel compelled to speak or write words to express themselves, then so be it, for it is what a person truly intends that will make the difference. Speaking and writing truth is the goal.

XXVII. Helping Nations

For decades, the current government of America has helped many nations to feed, clothe, and house themselves. America has sent armies to aide in their defense and have given technology to bring them into the future. Most despicably, this Nation has been racially and politically selective in its release of medical aid, food and technology to many other world populations. The current government of America, for many unknown and selfish reasons, has also instigated radical changes not in the best interest of the unsuspecting nations. This has resulted in the senseless murder by the receiving countries ruling class of many innocent men, women, and children with less than plausible explanations due to this fact.

We have already discussed the use of currency earlier in this text, and have come to realize that it really has no purpose in deciding the fate of humans, unless we believe it so.

Therefore, if we do not believe, it will eventually lead to our understanding. We will, however, still need to use it as a tool for a time to encourage others to carryout tasks important to establishing the new government.

We must help our Homeland America to regain its luster and dignity before we can be in a position to help others. America, too, is a nation needing help, and help we will give it, getting rid of the slums and other living conditions. Politics and ramblings of greedy business leaders trolling for profit have destroyed the art of helping. Programs currently underway to assist others will be evaluated for their trustworthiness and general intent. There are too many wolves in sheep's clothing wishing to take advantage of the unsuspecting to reap the benefits for themselves. The government of *The American Republic* will truly help those that are willing to help themselves if they can, and if not, we will teach them.

XXVIII.   Propaganda, Edward Bernay

Propaganda is a word that uses a set of words or actions that are either true or false when utilized for the benefit or to the detriment of someone. Propaganda does not prejudice itself to either one or to the many, as long as the primary objective has been accomplished.

Truth is truth. False is deception, without any concern or regard for the one or ones it is to directly or indirectly affect.

These techniques have been used for centuries to be triumphant in arguments, wars, and human involvements. The universal use of technology now places many tools in the hands of these global operatives who can be contracted to carry out any one of the multi-pronged tactics from a selected form of propaganda to wage an attack.

Paper and pen, word of mouth, false flag, covert operations, radio, television, the Internet, civil unrest, crowd gatherings, and even this Manifestum are all tools employed to convince the populace of an idea. The choice to make is, which idea truly benefits the many and not the few. However, it is vital for the survival of a nation, especially our America, that the current propaganda machine be ferreted out, dismantled, and destroyed.

XXIX. Volunteerism

This word denotes the sacrifice of one's self in the aide of another. To be able to freely offer one's precious time or life in the pursuit of assisting fellow citizens, is a wonderful way to live life.

Volunteerism is an endowment living within all of us, and this gift should only be given when the cause is just and true. To expect anything less than that would be a mockery to the word's true intent.

Governments currently use volunteerism as a way to bolster the number of troops in the military; or to save money on city and government projects; or to get something for nothing; or to just line their pockets with more gold. Their exploitation of citizens cheapens the true meaning of the word, and fewer Americans believe it as patriotic a thing to do as they once had. Either way, the act of volunteering must be reborn to mirror its original meaning and purposeful cause.

XXX. Terrorism and Treason

Terrorism exists everywhere, not just in some religious jihad. Every nation has terrorists residing within its own population.

Now, why have terror? It unfortunately depends upon the cause and or reason why that person or those persons decide to wreak havoc on a nation and its people.

During the early part of American history, Brettaniai likened Americans settlers to terrorists, because they rebelled against the ruling class, and distanced themselves from the system of government they believed to be unjust. Throughout time, the ruling party has always reasoned that anyone opposed to its rule could be no less that a terrorist. Terrorists have never survived in the open, and have always lived their lives rooting around underground or behind closed doors plotting their every move against those they oppose.

The government of *The American Republic* will never tolerate terrorists who terrorize Americans on American soil. They will be sought out and systematically destroyed. Terrorists will be the exception to the three-day rule of execution. Their deaths will be swift. If any family members can be tied in to a terrorist's treasonous activities, they too, will be labeled as traitors and subject to execution and/or banishment. American citizens they are not, and when captured, terrorists will suffer the most inhumane deaths. They will suffer ten-fold.

It is also realized that interlopers from other countries have influenced American citizens to carryout false flag operations that disrupt America and its commerce. This is treason.

The American Republic will ferret out the traitors who dare to blend with our own. When these chameleons are exposed and found guilty of treason by the American people, they too, will be severely punished under law like the terrorists they are.

There is no room for terrorist activity, unless however, it is brought on in response to a corrupt system of government and business that has brought harm to its citizens. If that were so, then it would be terrorism's purpose to free its people. Terrorism is not always violent.

There is a way to save innocent lives when engaged in this type of activity. Become like a surgeon selectively finding those who are the troublemakers. There should be no collateral damage to the innocent if a well-planned campaign is waged.

XXXI.   Weapons of Mass Destruction, WMD

America has in its arsenal of weaponry, an eclectic selection of devices that are considered WMD's. These weapons are considered quite dangerous and are not to be taken lightly when used as a threat for peace or resolving some other military plan.

For many centuries on planet earth, there have existed some of the most exotic weapons imaginable. Many of these weapons' designs date back many thousands of years, while scientists and engineers to this day, are still in a quandary as to their originators. It is no surprise that this technology is still being utilized to create weapons that are in use today. America surpassed every other Nation as the world's leader in creating extraordinary and innovative weaponries after World War II. Although most of this military technology has been kept hidden from the public, there are currently weapons in use on this planet that would overwhelm the average mind. The power this armament wields is unimaginable, and as a result, America will continue to be the global forerunner with its military weaponry design.

Designs exist of wartime weapons' technology, that when completely developed, would be more destructive than any other known to humankind. Their use against humankind would be cataclysmic.   Current bio-weaponry and nuclear military hardware would be no match against this new weapon and would give its owner complete domination over any nation.

However, if every nation possessed this weaponry of peace, it would produce the standoff needed to cease the wars and rumors of wars against one another. It would take this colossal threat to force populations into the realization that it is a human right to live together in peace.

The new government of *The American Republic* will encourage and insist that every nation act responsibly when it comes to the threat or eventual use of these weapons of mass destruction, no matter how devastatingly great or small. We, however, all are aware of the total annihilation that would occur if any one nation made the choice to open their battery of military hardware against the other. The world as we know it would cease to exist. As every nation continues to build its arsenal of weapons at a paranoid pace, the world must have in place the necessary security needed to maintain safe borders.

XXXII. Business

If a nation is to survive, it needs commerce. Business seems to be a vital component of human existence, and without it, humans cannot exist. Business protocols in place in America over the centuries has proven that commerce cannot be left in the hands of the wrong people.

The American Republic will see that every American will have the right and opportunity to own a community-based business. Every citizen should have the right to earn income and prosper in America, to catch the proverbial dream that has eluded him or her for so long. This dream will encourage the visionaries to seek out and fulfill their dreams, rather than becoming the work slaves of others.

America needs to reorganize its communities so that the citizens within learn to provide for themselves. People must have something to do with their lives, or they become either apathetic or complacent with the world around them. Bountiful resources waiting to be utilized can be found within every citizen. People are naturally willing to help carry out their neighbor's dreams as long as intentions remain honest and fair. This is why I repeat that people are a nation's most valuable resource. Private business is a privilege not a right. Americans would look to the new Congress to oversee private business concerns and grant licensing (Charters).

The American Republic advocates business as long as it does not stifle the creative and economic growth of the individual and the nation. Business leaders of today have forgotten the true meaning of business, which is to provide viable goods or services to the community without undue burden. A business' primary goal should not be about personal profits. Therefore, factories and other businesses that are counter to the earth's environment will not be allowed. Businesses not based on the needs of the community will not be considered for operation. If other communities wish to produce a particular product or service, they will have to prove their citizen's economic need for it.

Business growth should be determined by the needs of the community along with the quality of the goods and service, not thru trickery or false gimmicks.

America has lost its sprit of ingenuity and has exported itself to others without first taking into considerations the needs of Americans. It will be encouraged to build an American business into a thriving enterprise. No enterprise will continue to operate if it begins to evolve into some mega conglomerate that sucks the life-blood from the community and gives nothing back. The community will always be the most important part of any business, for without it the business would not be able to survive. The current government has allowed its business leaders to export our vital assets to other countries without regard or concern for the financial stability of our own Nation. This current government has prostituted itself to others for false promises and fleeting riches.

That in itself is a crime against humanity and to Americans. Every American will have an opportunity to decide what commerce is right for their nation. This will assure that our resources will never be allowed to be sold off to selfish people.

XXXIII.   Farming

Food sustains life on planet earth without exception. Farming is the lifeblood of any nation, for without it there would exist no people. America has vast lands to farm all varieties of foods for human consumption, and this real property must be brought under better supervision and control.

Business concerns are systematically destroying the farming instinct in Americans. There are generations of farming families in America that have fed America and other nations. Farmers have yet to be adequately compensated for their perseverance. Under *The American Republic* government, farming will be a priority, as will the American farmer. The government will not recognize the massive conglomerates of farming concerns that rape the farmer and the land without regard of the consequences to citizens and the environment. The Nationalization of the farming industry is necessary, however placing that control with the ones who have the experience and expertise is of utmost importance. This would be the farmer, because this is the person who is at one with the earth. Farming is not accomplished with a pen and paper. It is the one who tastes the earth, not the one that tastes the coffee in the office who should be in charge.

Farmers will get the respect and resources needed to be a farmer, without the fear of loss of land, crop, or animal. For too many years, American farmers have been methodically eliminated and replaced with large for-profit farming empires. The American farming industry will be re-established to feed Americans first, then the rest of planet earth if needed. America will lead the way in demonstrating to other nations how to adequately and equitably feed themselves first.

XXXIV. Abortion

It is the right of responsible women to make the choice either alone, with a spouse, parents, or legal guardian as to the fate of an unborn fetus at any stage of development. It is the responsibility of government to protect and defend that decision against any person interfering with that right of choice.

Religious zealots have no authority over this law and will not be allowed to influence any woman's right to choose. If that female permits their respective religion to determine her choice, then so be it. It remains the woman's choice.

Any prior rulings, nationwide, denying a woman's right to choose will not be recognized as law under the new government of *The American Republic*. This will be the law.

XXXV. Homosexuality

From the beginnings of human life on this planet, there has been this desire to have sexual relations with one another either for procreation or for pleasure.

Nature in its wisdom has allowed creation to take place between a male and a female. It has also given humans the desires and choices to decide through natural selection or personal choice, to have sexual relations with the same sex.

It is not wrong either way.   Religion and other convictions have other ideas on this subject, but they will not influence any government action on this topic.

Homosexuality is as old as we are, and is still accepted in many cultures on planet earth.

The government of *The American Republic* will defend the rights of its citizens whether they be homosexual or heterosexual. The new government is not and will not be homophobic.

Marriage is a public and private commitment between two people. If they are of the same sex, that will be acceptable under the new government of America, without prejudice. A person's sexuality is between themselves, their spouse or partner, and their religion. The government of *The American Republic* will protect the rights of all of its citizens no matter what differences they may have between each other, as long as they do not disrupt the government of America and abide by its laws. Too many people are ignorant of their ignorance, thus the problems and conflicts that ensue over the same sex issues.

XXXVI. Prostitution and Pornography

Prostitution and pornography have been an integral part of human culture for centuries and will no doubt be a part of American society for many more centuries to come.

The social and religious impact is of some concern of *The American Republic* because of the extent and nature of both. In other words, there will be limits to the extent that both can be fruitful and flourish. Prostitution between the two sexes is acceptable as long as it does not involve minor children below the age of 18 years. Any deviation from that will be dealt with severe punishment to all responsible parties. This also applies to any citizen's appetite for child pornography. No more children below the age of 18 years will be used to satisfy the sexual fantasies of those who prey on them. Heavy regulations on both industries will be the norm to control and punish those who do not follow the strict rules of law. The new government will not be able to stop what a person sees in their mind, but will be able to curtail it once they attempt to turn it into reality. Any Nation that attempts to import any illicit material into America that does not comply with current law will also be severely punished.

It is well understood that organizations that are "organized crime syndicates" will also have to follow the rules of law, even though they will be able to continue their control over this these types of industries under the watchful eye of government. Any outsiders who are not part of the newly formed commission will be dealt with thru law and punishment. Prostitution and pornography will become a legalized enterprise protected and overseen by law and a department of *The American Republic* government. There will be health, licensing, and other managing mechanisms to control this age-old human endeavor for pleasure.

XXXVII. Organized Crime

Since the inception of America, there have been people who have not had the best interests of the nation at heart. They have brought with them the instinct to survive in a system of deception and lies. These organizers have come from all ethnic and social backgrounds. They have infiltrated the very core of society and profited from its weaknesses.

They have used the failings of our citizens to spawn an enterprise of wealth, thru drugs, alcohol sex, and murder. They have controlled the very foundations of government and commerce which has led to a very different way for Americans.

American citizens know them for what they are and what they have done to transform the American society into one of co-dependence for sex, drugs, blackmail, extortion, slave trade, gambling, liqueur, food, entertainment, and many other profitable businesses that rely on the pleasures and desires of people. It would seem that these types of organizations would be a good litmus test for our Nation's weaknesses.

Unfortunately, American government and business leaders have fallen victims to these organized criminals who have cleverly exploited citizen's fears and weaknesses. The government of *The American Republic* fully understands the workings of these organized criminal enterprises that wreck havoc on the American society.

The new government will recruit strong-minded, well- disciplined citizens to fill the departments of government appointed to control these Gangs of America.

If anyone violates that trust and becomes influenced by any organized criminal group or gang, they will be severely punished along with the organized criminal group or gang that conspired with or perpetrated the crime.

Organized gangs have plagued America for centuries, and they will continue as long as any government allows it. The current government has ignored gang activities because they have been beneficial in business dealings. That will cease in *The American Republic*. Once the financial motivation is removed, the gangs will have no need to organize. If they choose to continue without the benefits of monetary gain, they can only co-exist with the Government if there are clearly defined rules between the two. However, if any organized gang cannot come to a reasonable agreement, then they and all of their offspring will be ferreted out and destroyed.

XXXVIII.   Viriato, Hai Bà Trưng, Boadicea, Shaka kaSenzangakhona

It is extremely important to note that in order for the new government (*The American Republic*) to take form, the American Military with The People must support the change of government.

It would not be impossible to replace the current system of government in America if all Americans, including its military forces, joined in solidarity to overcome the current ruling class to replace it with one that is truly for the benefit of the many and not the self-selected few.

The world is watching and waiting for that group of citizens to convince the military and the citizens of America to replace the current government in America to rid the land of all who wish to serve themselves and not The People.

There have been many great warriors through the ages who took on what had been deemed the impossible task of throwing off their oppressors. These brave men and women faced even greater armies who had once forced them into submission under a government that no longer respected its people.   These governments had great strength, but lacked the wisdom and insight to truly understand the rightful place their citizens had earned. The formation of these governments was inspired by greedy humans to gain control of those citizens who were ignorant as to the true nature of their leaders. Thus, we witness the current collapse of America and the rest of the world.

I have written many words to express my point of view based on my years of observations, direct influence from outsiders, and involvement with earth's cycle.

We as a nation of people will see no other choice but to take action to make changes to rid ourselves of the tyranny that has been affecting us all. If it means the sacrificing of our lives then it shall be so, for life is not life if it cannot flourish in its own land. To give one's life so that another can live is the greatest sacrifice one can make. In addition, it is this ultimate sacrifice that sadly, many citizens may have to make if they are to see that the current system of government in America be replaced.

America needs honest people who will use truth to overcome all obstacles, resolve their ways and do what is right for others, not just America but the rest of planet earth.

This Manifestum is written for those people looking for a real change in their government: one that can satisfy all needs of The People and its citizens, without the rhetoric. For centuries, Americans have been yearning for a system of government to free them from their fears and insecurities. Strong, honest, and direct leadership is the only way to overcome the many obstacles that have been placed before most of us in America.

We all live in a Nation and on a planet that has fallen victim to those who are bent on doing harm to us all, without regard to the immediate or future outcomes of their behaviors. In order to maintain a compliant society, our current government along with its military cronies has allowed business interests to continue to dictate and manipulate the laws to their advantage. This will be turned around.

There will undoubtedly be those who will instigate reverse insurrection through false propaganda and fear, thus the potential death of many innocent citizens at the hands of the current military, freelance mercenaries, agency, and law enforcement. Those supporting *The American Republic* will do whatever humanly possible to minimize those losses.

As mentioned earlier, it will be up to the military of America to decide if it wishes to follow this Manifestum with the full support of American citizens. Without the support of both, this Manifestum is but words on paper with no purpose.

We are all humans first; the rest of our attributes have been gained through our own perseverance. Under *The American Republic* government, all people will have an equal chance to be what they wish, without the fear of failure. Parents will be more confident in seeing that their children succeed in life. They will posses newer skills that will provide them the tools and wisdom to get to those goals. This is in the plan of our new government. The Government of *The American Republic* will provide, without prejudice, the guidance and wisdom needed to become free spirited citizens who will, in turn, be able to provide for their planet earth, demonstrating to us all that there does exist a chance to be seen and known.

XXXIX.   OUR LAND, Manifest Destiny

Our Land, our America, was stolen from those who sought to share it with us all. Our ancestors came to America with the intent of fleeing the tyranny that ravaged them all abroad. Some came for religious freedoms, others for fortune, and others for reasons we will always ponder. However, they came, nonetheless with visions of freedom from their oppressors.

We are a people of this planet, and of this Nation called America; we are a people who will return to the Republic that was intended from the start. There was once a time when we were given the right of choice and freedom, without the restraints of self-serving laws. *The American Republic* is an idea that has been patiently waiting to come to fruition for all peoples of America, and eventually to the rest of planet earth.

What rights do we have as Peasants of *The American Republic*, Our Land? I have purposely not included the names of those individuals who contributed to our fledgling nation for good reason; they, themselves became infected with hypocrisy, fear and lies.

The American Republic Bill of Rights: (incomplete)

Every American will have freedom of speech and of the press or private writings.

Every American will have the right to a free and purposeful education without prejudice, with no more private, for-profit institutions of higher learning.

Every American will have the right to own/operate a community-based business without fear of corporate or hostile takeover. *The American Republic* will promote pride of honest ownership.

Every American will have the right and privilege to own a home with land, thus eliminating the need for rag-tag apartments and other crowded dwellings.

Every American will have the right to free health care. Healthcare will no longer be run as a for-profit, private business. A healthy Nation breeds healthy results.

Every American will have the right to practice his or her respective religious beliefs, as long as it does not overtly encroach upon another's belief, or threaten another citizen with violence.

Every American will have the right to have a retirement fund provided by government.

Every American will have the right to farm if it benefits his family and thriving community businesses.

Every American will have the right to be protected by law enforcement. Every American will have the right to protection under the original Bill of Rights that was included in the original Constitution.

Every American will have the right to contribute ideas for improvement to the Republic.

Every American will have the right to redress differences to the Republic through the new Congress, rather it be State or local.

Every American will have the right to participate in government.

Every American will have the right to change for the good of themselves and for the good of humankind.

These are but a few of the rights that *The American Republic* believes every American and every human being on planet earth should have protected. Every human being has inalienable rights that are part of the human spirit.

XL. Pflichterfüllung

It is the duty and the responsibility of every American and in fact, every human being on planet earth to correct the wrongs, defend the innocent, and make a more environmentally habitable world. When this is accomplished, we as humans will send a visible message to those who have been watching over us for so many millions of years. This message will communicate that we are ready to take a step forward in evolution, and move into the paradigm of truth. America must be the leader in this quest for change that will eventually spark a transformation for the entire planet. It is, however, so unfortunate that so many of us are still being cleverly duped in believing that our current system of thought is the only way for us to live. Americans have unknowingly allowed those who promoted this change to trick us into believing this mass propaganda. Only more recently have we discovered their words to be fraught with lies and deceit. Yet here we citizens sit, caught in the middle of our sinkhole of an economy trying to survive on dim promises.

In the future, these traitors of the truth will be identified and eliminated without mercy, for the pain and suffering that they and their descendants have placed upon all of those living in this, our nation. These acts of treason upon the citizens of America, their very neighbors, have been reprehensible.

When America becomes the first to change, that is when a clear message will be sent to other nations that this Nation will no longer tolerate dissension in its government and commerce. It is now time for Americans to break the chains that hold us from seeking this truth so that we can move forward in a direction that will bring us all into a lifestyle that will benefit the whole rather than the privileged few. We have allowed these "invisible" puppeteers to manipulate and control our everyday lives, without the slightest regard to our outcome. Americans can no longer be slaves of their government, for we are a life form that has evolved like no other life form that exists on this planet. It is the "magic" of nature that has transformed us into the creatures we have become, today.

Propaganda specialists have been craftily utilizing our own information networks to further manipulate the masses into becoming a society of "drones." The news media has been nurtured into a mass distributor of Babel as it moves along in its quest of flimflamming and betraying the American people. In addition, do not forget our present military, for it too, has been fashioned into a tool to further control The People. Their leaders continually spin tale after tale of propagandist waste which is lapped up hungrily by unwary citizens.

It is for these reasons that everything represented by the current American system must be replaced with *The American Republic* system of government that will represent The People of this nation as their true protector.

We The People of America are suffering the deepest humiliation in this nation's history, and we are sadly, reaping what we have allowed to be sowed. Every American must be able believe in their government again. Without this, America will not be able to survive another generation. People need people, and without this kinship, humans would wander aimlessly into extinction.

Unfortunately, there will be those that will oppose this new idea of government and will utilize every "trick" known to humans to dislodge it from the minds of the many. It is your duty as an American and as a human being to stand together as one nation to deflect the onslaught of the shadow government that has plagued humans for centuries. These undetectable governors of hypocrisy have been manipulating the system of law, government, business, and our daily lives for too long. They have led us to believe through their propagandist tactics that in order to be a patriotic American we must adhere to their rules of law. Americans know all too well the ultimate penalties for not abiding by these rules of law: alienation, imprisonment, humiliation, torture, and death.

XLI.   Humans are The Dream of Dolphins

Wouldn't be nice to be able to walk amongst the animal kingdom, without the fear of capture, enslavement, and death? Is it possible to be able to live amongst ourselves without fear?

Can you imagine a world where everyone works together to build a place for all to enjoy?

Can you imagine a government that can truly provide for The People it is supposed to govern and serve?

Can you imagine owning land and a home without the fear of loss?

Can you imagine what it would be like to worship your religion in peace?

Can you imagine the planet cared for by humans who comprehend the dynamics of planet earth and who are capable of protecting it?

Can you imagine a military that truly defends the interests of The People and not just a select few?

Can you imagine the response from earth's People when full disclosure is made about the existence of other beings and how their planet's technology and philosophy has influenced our planet for millennia?

Under the new government we Americans will be able to dream again and become The People the dolphin's dream of us becoming.

XLII.   The Undiscovered Nation

American Republic 2012, AMR 2012 is the date that has been chosen to instigate change for a new government for The People of America. This gives you, the reader, an opportunity from now until that point in time to make your decision for this change. If you are reading this Manifestum after AMR 2012, it is hoped that the change has already taken place and this document has become historical.

Americans: who are all peoples residing in American territories at the time of this change will become part of this new revolutionary change in government. This transformation will be the third event in American history where an insurrection of thoughts and ideas has been set into action in order to free the enslaved minds of citizens who have been tricked by the government's cunning ploys. It is vital for the very survival of the human race that all Americans stand together in solidarity and fight off those who have designed this thinly veiled lifestyle that we all have become accustomed too. Physiological debate with no action has allowed this deceptive system of misinformation to mass manipulate our minds into confusion. Just look around and witness the poisonous grasp these purveyors of power have on all who live and speak in our America. The inception of this new idea of the government of *The American Republic* is the only veritable means for achieving the guaranteed freedoms our citizens have long deserved. The idea of a new government is not new; it is a method of de-controlling The People, by The People. This new government will be a government of trust.

The stress of everyday life has been systematically tearing most Americans apart. Only a minute few have squeezed thru the very small tunnel of success to warrant some acknowledgement. Those remaining outside the circle of hope have suffered through complex social stresses that only can be experienced by those existing within the lower ring of our society's human cast system.

How many American citizens have truly assimilated into today's society of humans?

How many American citizens have been divided into a system of phyla?

How many American citizens reading this Manifestum truly understand the world they live in?

How many American citizens have become so apathetic or so given up on their lives that they have become drones in society's pecking order?

How many American citizens were at one time or another judged based upon race, color, gender, or any human frailty?

How many American citizens throughout time have lost their lives because of the ignorance of other people? Your government has forsaken you all and a revolution for change must come. The People who "HAVE" have no desire to change, but their numbers pale in comparison to the numbers of those who "HAVE NOT." These citizens still outnumber those who keep them enslaved in lies and this will become their ultimate advantage. Do not underestimate us.

The American Military must first read this Manifestum, then discuss and ask questions before any action can be taken to compel any magnitude of change. Once leaders of the armed forces realize the truths within, then and only then can the next steps towards reforming our current system of government take place.

We implore the rank and file of the military to stand with us, for we are militia, as well, we are your family. No aggression, just knowing.

Remember the countless wars that have been fought for reasons other than intended?

Remember the tears shed when loved ones never returned from battle?

Look to 2012.

2012 will be a year for all of humankind to focus on. Americans are also aware that with this date, comes predictions by a race of people whose calendar comes to an end, that life, as we know it will end in recognition of a new one that will begin.

Will this be the end of the world, as we know it?

No, it is not.

It will be the beginning of another nation, another world.

It will be the becoming of a new America.

It will be the birth of a genuine opportunity for change.

Let me state again, that it is crucial that our Armed Services fully comprehend what we are asking for: to free The People of America from the bondage of a corrupt system of government. We all can become soldiers for change and tip the scale in favor of The People.

XLIII. Public Apology to Women of the World from
The American Republic (Hypatia of Alexandria)

Before we begin our campaign, we would like for all women of this planet

to please find it in their hearts to forgive the pain, death and disrespect that

we men have caused you for so many thousands of years. Our arrogance

and ignorance has regrettably fostered this gender separation generation

after generation. Women are the greatest treasure the earth has given us,

yet many still refuse to recognize or even appreciate what gifts you bring to

this planet. Our religions and politics have historically restricted your

voices, your creativity, and your minds. You have been programmed to

believe that you must submit to our will. That is not true. Women are our

equals, our other half of reason, our companions for eternity. It is our

responsibility to care for you, respect you, and love you as ONE. Women

will never be looked upon as second-class persons.

We of *The American Republic* will not allow anyone, male or female; to

ever degrade a woman's status as a human being or tolerate misogyny. We

will protect you from whatever stands in your way, and respectfully

include you in the design of the new Republic. WE will fight for the

unconditional freedom of Women to be free from the invisible chains and

glass ceilings that impede your intellectual, social, economical, and

political growth. In *The American Republic*, women will no longer suffer

the stigma of only being subjects of man's carnal desire. In *The American*

Republic, women will have the same dignity and respect due all humans regardless of their lifestyle or intelligence. As with all American citizens, class or race will not segregate women, all will be welcomed without regard of status or place of origin.

Nature created us all to exist as one in peace, and care for our home planet earth, and so it shall be.

XLIV. Proletariat

Wageworkers and those earning a meager salary are the citizens we call out to. For without their daily struggle to make ends meet, the rest of America would find it less comfortable. Who keeps America running for the wealthy? YOU DO!. Who enlists in the armed forces risk life and limb to defend America while only earning paltry compensation? YOU DO! Who is subject to inequitable taxation and outrageous pricing for goods and services, while controllers of government and commerce get fatter and richer? YOU ARE!

The rights of American Citizens must be guaranteed and protected to those who work so hard to provide for themselves and their families. They should be able to guiltlessly reap the benefits of the bountiful resources existing in America without fear of reprisal.

Under new government, everyone will have the opportunity to live in a supportive neighborhood where the needs of the many, as well as the few will be met, through the collective and collaborative work of that community.

XLV. The Children

What about the children? What do we do about the young humans who are suffering alongside the adults?

In most cases, children have no idea of the chaos churning around them, because their parents and teachers have been shielding them from it. More recently, our children have been faced with monumental instances of despair, homelessness, lack of stable family units, and lack of parental control or love. What is most disturbing is the current government's underlying lack of concern. Our children's futures are dependent upon the illusory promises of adults they have been conditioned to trust. They are being subjected to a society of smoke and mirrors, and will never know whom to trust.

What has the current system of government in America done to protect its children? Not as much as they should have considering the plight of America's young people. *The American Republic* will address this issue immediately. There will not be one child in America left to suffer the atrocities that adult citizens have allowed to flourish. In America, if we have more than one child who is without, then that will be considered unacceptable.

Until they can survive on their own, children with or without parents will be offered support. The government will naturally assist its children and assure that they are housed, fed, clothed, and educated, because it is they who will ultimately govern this Nation.

The American Republic will always be there for its citizens, whether they

be children or adult. Without children a nation cannot flourish, thus the

importance of protection by government without prejudice.

Children are the future of the human race on planet earth, and will be given

that opportunity to carry on as was promised by those who came long

before us. They are the light and the salvation of humankind for the

present and the future.

XLVI.   A New Republic, A Point of View, Sūn Wǔ, Chibi

My life will never be the same.

Now is the time for all good women and men to come to the aid of their Nation, their Homeland, their America.

Readers, you must search inside your very being and discover your truth. Do not rely entirely on this Manifestum or any other philosophical treatise on right and reason. Use the common sense that is embedded in your genetic structure. Use your human intuition to ask yourself if you are completely satisfied with your life on this planet.

I realize that there are some people who believe that if they posses enough worldly "things" it will be sufficient to satisfy them in their current lifestyle. Nevertheless, those material possessions are lacking the innermost fulfillment needed to let them truly enjoy the entire life experience.

This Manifestum is directed to every reader, of every origin, without prejudice. In order for the words in this document to make any sense, it is vitally important for you, the reader of this Manifestum, to take your time to completely digest what has been written.

Our planet, our home, has been given to us by those wishing only the best for us all, and what have we done with it over the millennium? The earth's ecological system now hangs in a precarious balance between sustainability and extinction; pollution has been steadily converting the very air we breathe into a noxious gaseous mixture; our water has become so tainted by unregulated factory runoffs that communities have become fatally sickened; and our natural resources, worldwide, are being ravenously devoured by greedy industry czars. In addition, all of these horrors have been slowly unfolding under the averted eyes of global governments. These are the same governments, dictatorships, kingships, and authoritative control systems that have maintained ultimate control over the world's populous with no moral accountability

We can write voluminous treatises philosophizing upon the whys of the world's plights, but to what end? No one is willing to take the first step, blow the first whistle, or shed the first blood.

Too many discourses have been written by far too many individuals who have been skillfully intertwining the political and economical circumstances to cleverly conceal American citizens' primary goal of freedom and justice. These powerful leaders have been at work for centuries, positioning themselves for their ultimate objective of controlling the American inhabitants, and then on to the global populations. Fortunately, there are far too many humans on planet earth for that long-term master plan to be immediately carried out. However, citizens cannot rest on that presumption. This is your wake-up call.

The powers that be have realized long ago that it is easier to control a population of millions rather than billions, and so the selective process of careful and pre-meditative elimination of humans. There exists now a systematic reduction of the human population on planet earth through well-placed diseases, planned wars, instigated mayhem, and other human-made causes. For those who sit in authority on planet earth and in America, genocide and biocide have become most effective tools. Control is also being accomplished by shifting the earth's resources so that countries pay their debts with their own people, in place of capital. The national debt is an illusion.

The American Republic believes that by gathering the right kindling within the mind of the reader, this Manifestum will be the very accelerant needed to set their thoughts on fire. Once this fire is started, it will be impossible to put it out. It will become the eternal flame of truth!

When the military troops of America read this Manifestum and re-examine the Intel being fed to them, they will rethink sacrificing their lives in defense of this Nation's current leaders. We are aware that many leaders in the military have philosophically taken an oath of allegiance to defend the interests of America. We are also aware that they symbolically report to and take orders from the Commander in Chief, the President of America. The reality, however, is much different, because American Presidents no longer actually lead their troops into war.

As stated before, it is of no use for Americans to rise up and demand a change in their government if they do not have the complete support of the military forces. Without that strength, any attempt by citizens to gain control of the government will be fraught with violence.

The paradox: so which side is right?

Honor, Integrity, Loyalty, Duty, Respect, Selfless Service, Courage, Commitment, are but words on paper used to beguile those fresh young minds into a mindset of dedication and loyalty. These false promises of freedom and justice for all are devised to lure recruits into the willingness to lose their life, without regard. *The American Republic* will not use lies to justify a means to an end, as the current government does. *The American Republic* will only speak truths to its soldiers of *The American Republic* Army.

I write with conviction and purpose because of my firm belief in the progress humans on this planet deserve. The ones in power have the ability to write history anyway they wish without much contention. In addition, if contested, it is propagandized as conspiracy. It is crucial, however, to start this change in America. There undoubtedly will be those who will scoff at the idea of a revolution in America and will attempt to perpetuate their fears and insecurities upon the innocent as they lay blame elsewhere.

Every American citizen must have the ability to make the choice for change without fear of retaliation. Citizens will have the right to dissent from any ideas being proposed, but when it is evident that the current system of thought is keeping Americans from what is right, it will be imperative that the current system of rights be reconstituted. When that time arises, those dissenters either must get on board or will be removed. Once Americans make that choice to live free and prosper, there will be help from those who have nudged us along for so many centuries. The entire planet needs Americans to make the change first, so the cure for the disease of ignorance can be eradicated. Those holding power on planet earth are afraid of this Manifestum of ideas, because it means the eventual end of their rule over The People and the ushering in of those who have been silent for so long. Who are the silent ones, you ask? They are the caretakers of the truth, the ones who began enlightening, and illuminating the truths to humans from humankind's beginnings.

There will be no prerequisite to receive the specific knowledge they intend to impart, other than the desire to become wise, as did our ancestors. Traditionally, our schools of thought believed it to be in our best interest to pre-select what truths to teach the masses. This has been a deceitful practice. In *The American Republic*, there must be and will be an honest exchange of dialogue between The People in every language, so that all can be educated and included in all decision-making. Once The People have the ability to comprehend what their changed America will do for them, a well-defined Republican form of government will be on its way into being.

In order to facilitate this change to our America, a frank demonstration of unprecedented power will be the only method required to compel those in power to relinquish their death-grip on our lands. Those in power will have to make a choice to either step away from the reigns of the government and commerce to let the American people rebuild their nation, or face annihilation.

The original architects of the first Manifestum for America wrote it for that era, never anticipating that their political descendants would govern with selfish control for centuries beyond. Ignorance has been our worst enemy and that has been what has kept Americans from the truth.

The current powers have depended upon our ignorance, and have been very busy positioning themselves to be the ultimate rulers of our land and our planet.

The irony: this is happening with the unbridled consent of citizens.

There is no other way to overcome our corrupt system of government without complete acquiescence by every American. Be reminded that it is not impossible to obtain change, it is only difficult, and there is always a cost. This was accomplished before in the 1700's and took many years to mature, but positive changes did eventually come about with the government. Unfortunately, there were still those who did not fully comprehend the total concept of freedom and liberty, for all. That is how women wound up with the short end of the stick with being valued less than their male counterparts. Slavery and genocide were also accepted realities by most of the signers of the document of independence which is contradictory to the intent. You can never have a successful society without both women and men working together as a cohesive team. History has proven that without that balance there will always be discord. Discord was the perfect and carefully planned distraction used to trick the American people into opening the city gates and welcoming in those whose promises would not be kept. However, within all of that orchestrated confusion, citizens were completely bamboozled, and before they knew what hit them, they were under absolute domination by a corrupt system of rule.

Look around you, Americans, and see for yourself. Do not put your head into the sand and hope that it will have all gone away by the time you look up. Action with a well-planned goal will motivate Americans into change. Citizens must all carefully think this out, because it will not take religious conviction to save America from this evil. To break the chains of ignorance and vanquish the powers that be, will require the power of all The People acting as one, not God, to move in the direction of truth. There are so many decisions we must make, but the most crucial is to make this change and to make this change now!

There is little left of "The American Way." The current system of government has definitely made sure of that.

The commanders of our Armed Services are not true to their covenant of defending our land from those who will move in and disrupt our way of life. In fact, they have literally opened America's doors to welcome them in, without so much as a pat down. It is the right and duty of every American to look to the military to cast these interlopers out.

Most of American interests have been sold off to non-Americans, hence, our current financial dilemma. Employment is prostituted offshore, unions are being methodically abolished or broken down, and greed has resulted in the diminished quality of manufactured goods so that profit margins soar even higher. The American worker has been reduced to a customer service representative, and consumers have become product testers. Inferior goods are flowing into our Nation as fast as their filthy factories can produce them. As long as an unchecked government remains in bed with the commerce whore, the public will continue to be sickened more than ever. So would you like to more?

All things considered, re-read this Manifestum, and discuss it with your peers. Ask even more questions of each other. Question the true duties of the military, and ask them to support your freedom. Once everyone has made that final choice to change the government, then it will be the time to move into a true Republican system.

This is just the beginning of the start of a new civilization developing in America. There will undoubtedly be those who will oppose this radical change in government, as they did during the foundation of our nation in the 1700's. It took many years to come up with a solution that pleased the masses, and eventually came about during active conflict with America's oppressor.

Those humans making up the "shadow government" are ultimately controlling us all. However, even they must realize that they have but a limited time to make the decision to give in or die fighting. Historically, the later will be the most likely result when evidencing the results of past revolts.

American society has been fooled into believing that what exists today in America is the only way for this Nation to progress into the future. Citizens have been manipulated into believing that any deviation from this carefully cultivated path will lead to complete discord in this Nation and the removal of their so-called freedoms. How much more wool can they pull over American citizens' eyes?

There are people who have the answers to all of your questions sitting in protective environments undaunted by your cries for help. We know who these people are. When they are told of the existence of this Manifestum, what will they do? Will they reveal themselves in defense against the eventual onslaught of questions and threatened uprisings? On the other hand, will they tunnel deeper into their protective government-funded catacombs in order to concoct more lies to spew upon our citizens?

They are quite aware of what truth can do, thus their fear. We will use their own techniques of truth to tear down their walls of deception. We will utilize the assistance of those beings that have been watching earth for centuries. They will be summoned to effectuate the transformation in the way of life on this planet that they have always envisioned for us humans. America will be the great Nation with a new freedom and liberty for all, without prejudice to the weak, the poor, the less educated, or the innocent. Demagogy remains a divisive government strategy being widely used by those individuals possessing an understanding of its deep psychological and controlling effects on the masses. The continued telling of lies to those who cannot immediately ascertain the difference has systemically destroyed the very foundation of American beliefs. Banning its strategic use on The People of this planet would result in a better-informed and trusting people. It will, however, take many years to garner the trust again in Americans after being subjected to the political rhetoric by their elected leaders for so many centuries.

True sovereignty is an earthly right granted to all human beings, as long as it is kept in tune with common and natural laws. It was attempted in America long ago, and was almost a success until the wrong intents and purposes took control of the entire system of ruling.

So, if given a choice to make your lifestyle better, which government would you choose?

Would it be a system of government that can only offer you the current and misleading system of thought? Alternatively, will it be the system of government that is offered in this Manifestum of ideas?

The eventual choice will be for you the reader to decide. Think of those who have no concept what has been going on around them, or what lies have been fed them. This Manifestum is meant to give you a glance into what has been kept from your eyes for far too long. This Manifestum is designed to stir up in you, the passion that your ancestors once reigned down upon their oppressors.

In order to challenge and overcome any conflicting plan, you must counter it with a proposal that can withstand any attack from those wishing not to give it credence. This emerging idea must include all parties at first, because the truth will eventually weed out any naysayers still clinging to the old thoughts. They will be dealt with accordingly.

A leader of men and women is an important role to accept, especially when so many lives are at stake. The new leader of *The American Republic* will most certainly see that decision-making will directly affect The People not only in America, but also around the world. When citizens stop living as ill-informed followers casually taking commands from those who have stolen the truth, their eyes will finally focus on the realities of this nation. Historically, this focus always comes far too late for people to recognize that their trusted leader's mesmerizing babble was only employed to trick them, yet again. This will no longer be the American way.

A true leader always tells the truth, and rarely, if at all, requires protection.

A true leader makes no compromise with those who do not have the best interest for The People.

A true leader provides freedom and sustenance for all.

A true leader can move within the lands without fear, and is respected, even by an enemy.

A true leader can freely call to the citizens for discipline and sacrifice.

A true leader will believe that The People can accomplish the impossible.

WE call on all Americans to hold another convention of Congress to start a new government for all peoples of America, and to do so without the consent of the current government.

You ask, "How do we start?" *The American Republic* will start with this Manifestum of ideas. This will not be an easy task to accomplish, but if the military along with a significant percentage of citizens compel this change, then this Nation's original covenant of a trusting government will come to fruition.

People who have accumulated power and wealth will find it very difficult to part with that status. This self-centered mentality to maintain societal standing has been engrained in Americans for generations, and will be a hard nut to crack. A decision for change will have to come from every citizen, even those who have been desensitized to the plight of the Nation for so many generations.

When citizens of America do finally assemble the courage to break the government's constraints on their freedom of thought, those who have maintained that power over them will fall from their ivory towers of control, and run in fear. Know this, that the powers that be running America could care less about the final outcome of your lives. Remember that we are all nobilis without question, and it is this fact that we must all begin to quickly realize. No man or woman in America has ever been less worthy than those in power, only less informed. In addition, keeping citizens cowering beneath it all has been the government's well-oiled plan for every man, woman, and child in America. The "Blue Blood" nom de plume has been just another age-old device used by those in power to make citizens believe that some divine influence anointed them to be the definitive rulers of the land. Now our eyes have been opened wide to their ruse, in the wake of our materialization.

Look around you and do not waiver, for we must all make some great sacrifice in order to realize victory. There will be help from others once they see the numbers of us moving forward to take action. If we are to be taken seriously by anyone, then we must make that initial effort to change ourselves first, then our America will fall into place. This advancement will finally prove that we as humans are ready to begin the journey to the stars.

Once people can accept the reality of this change, they will come to realize that we all live in the same house, just in different rooms. When that realization manifests itself worldwide, then we can all truly become the Human Race!

XLVII.   NOVUS ORDO SECLORUM, THOMAS PAINE

Now is the time for all good men and women to come to aid of their

Nation!

XLVIII.   Zeitgeist, Genius seculi

KNOW THYSELF γνῶθι σεαυτόν **gnōthi seauton**

This Manifestum is a perfect idea written by an imperfect human being.

We are not afraid of the TRUTH, are you?

We are a Legion of many, who will live a life of peace, with respect for all

living things. We will see value in those who are not exactly like us, and

look for ways to truly accommodate and educate those who are slow to

understand the change.

We will be an emerging nation of people encouraging anyone, anywhere to

become part of *The American Republic!*

"A Republic, if you can keep it" - Benjamin Franklin

"Reason obeys itself; and ignorance submits to whatever is dictated to it."- Thomas Paine

"Educate and inform the whole mass of the people...They are the only sure reliance for the preservation of our liberty."   Thomas Jefferson

"We, the people are the rightful masters of both Congress and the courts, not to overthrow the Constitution, but to overthrow men who pervert the Constitution." Abraham Lincoln

The American Republic

"Oh Lord, My God, is there no help for the widow's son?"

XLIX.   Philosophical Miscellany

- For those who know of the holidays remember as a child the strong belief in that day, the conviction of truth, the joy of that jubilee and all of its benefits. Remember the anticipation of that day, the days, and weeks leading up to that glorious day? You really believed didn't you? The entire town was in the moment; there was peace and harmony.

Government can be as that day was to those that can remember, except this time there will not be the disappointment when you found out the truth, that the jubilee you celebrated was only a tradition or myth.

- *The American Republic* will bring back the hopes and dreams of the past and put a smile on everyone's face without the tears of unhappiness.

- Problems are opportunities to solve for all Americans without regard to social class.

- *The American Republic* has made the decision to make changes to government only.

- Religion will change once the truth is known.

- Corruption within local government has raped the land.

- Chasing the dream and not the competition will eventually be the norm.

- Business moguls that have prostituted America and its ideas to others for profit and control have clouded the idea of American ingenuity.

- When another human touches another human by force without consent, it is a crime. There are levels of human touch, some out of love and affection, or by accident within close proximity. There are other forms of touch that cause bodily harm physically and emotionally and these are defined under law, and if not will have to be.

- The enforcement of laws is in itself, a science.

- Technology will continually be upgraded at all times.

- The safety of all Americans is of paramount concern of the government without exception.

- Americans are not beasts of burden, and will not have to suffer the pain of loss and fear from any financial institution.

- There are millions of ideas that if properly nurtured can become a reality and come to fruition.

- A strong family can help save the neighborhood of others.

- Humans control the lives of other creatures on planet earth, without their consent, this will cease.

- Humans have derived a method to choose another to become the judge of the law that in turn imposes its decision over the one it applies to.

- No one person on earth is perfect to perfection, thus we must understand that we are humans and not perfect. We must learn to forgive one another and forget in order to obtain that bliss that exists in all of us.

- Natural law has its own set of rules that must be adhered to.

- If a system of government is not true to its word, then it, too, must suffer the fate of belief from The People. That belief will destroy it, modify it, or accept it without question.

- Humans have a chance to evolve into a new form, not in the body, but in the spirit.

- Freedom is not just a philosophical concept, but an inherit human trait that is part of natures wonderful ballet.

- Using humans as testing grounds for new weapons and scientific potions will cease.

- If others challenge us as a nation in a less than an appropriate way, then we will naturally respond in defense of our interests.

- Any lost sheep (Americans) will be found and returned to the flock.

- We cannot blame any so-called illegal aliens that currently live in America for our demise, for there are terrorists that are Americans robbing this Nation of its resources, which in turn destroys the lives of so many Americans.

- We realize that there are those that are not considered legal citizens of America, and will be dealt with.

- Let us not concern oneself about another person who breaks bread on one end other than your end.

- A business concern should be established to provide a product or service to the community that it resides in.

- Treachery exists in all forms of government, people, and business concerns. That is unacceptable, and will not be tolerated under the new rule of law.

- For centuries the experiment of long ago has taken a different course than what was planned, thus our current and past demise.

- Just because someone has never experienced an educational institution, doesn't t mean that person is ignorant. If one has never experienced a trade, does not mean that person is ignorant either.

- Gifts for America for the First Americans.

- Every American will have the right to a legal representative to defend in a criminal case or any other legal matter without worry of cost.

- Every American will have the right to life or death as long as it does not directly affect another, and is rightfully justified, not instigated for reasons of prejudice, or any other unlawful act.

- Every American has the right to be saved in case of world disaster.

- For reason of faith, every American will have the opportunity to believe in their religion.

- Government will not be operated by religion.

- There is no "Mandate of Heaven" there is only the TRUTH.

- How many "schools" of thought have been written down and debated?

- What have other countries done to protect their children? Not a few, but every child?

- We all were once children, some of us were fortunate to have the benefits that society rations out to those that comply with the rules of law, and then there are those that do not, or cannot by some quirk of fate. If given the opportunity to truly excel in a society without the fear of failure, you will most likely find that more humans will become better people and of course better citizens.

- Look at the religions that have induced membership based on fear, greed, and ignorance. Religious convictions have historically influenced people's separation from one rule of authority to another. This will not happen again.

- Look at what battles have been fought throughout history that led to some victories but even many more losses of life, land, and liberty.

- Ask The People of America what they truly wish for themselves and their families?

- It is very important that when communicating to Americans, the word should be understood by the majority of its citizens in American. People wishing to be part of the change of our Homeland and planet earth must not be excluded because of illiteracy.

- Immigrants who invaded the lands of the indigenous humans who inhabited this land thru crafty powers of persuasion and force took the lands from those that held these lands for centuries.

- America by fact is the largest consumer of goods and services than any other nation on planet earth. This reason alone is why America has been chosen to be the leader in the most radical change in history, since the revelation realized that other creatures exist in the universe. There are so many schools of thought on this planet. It seems impossible to sift thru finding the one idea that will allow all humans to live in peace. There is however, a clue, a government that truly provides for the safety, security, and freedom of its people by providing an environment for all to flourish.

- How many Americans truly understand the reasons for the revolution in America in the 1700's?

- Every American that lives within its borders will have the right to pursue their dreams, supported by *The American Republic* government.

- English is not the only language spoken on planet earth, or in America.

- More than a million people in America really need help. That fact alone makes those that have worked so long to control the entire population a bit nervous.

- America is supposed to be the land of the free and of the brave, so why it is not so, from everyone's point of view?

- Racial ignorance, social ignorance, and intellectual ignorance, has led to the current system of government and of thought not only in America, but the rest of planet earth.

- As mentioned before you cannot have religion and government work together especially for the common good of all.

- What is your ethnicity? An American is your answer. Why spend time and energy on cataloging people by the color of their skin or culture. When the day is over every human being on planet earth is interconnected by the elements of the stars.

- A Word is a spoken sound given meaning by others or by the source. All living beings use sounds and words to communicate with each other. A word has no intrinsic value other than what is given to it by the source or those that receive it.

- Truth is the absence of untruth.

- Life is abundant in the entire universe without special considerations given for anything other than what is planned by the collisions of particles of matter, and its dance with the energy that surrounds it.

- Armies are made up of people like you that have families and friends, so why the confusion? Armies are not some magical force, they are humans like you and I.

- If every able body American wishes to become a soldier and join *The American Republic* Army, then you will witness a shift in power from those that have it now, to those that we choose to manage our Homeland and eventually our planet.

- Lying is a vice that must be overcome. If you begin to tell the truth no matter the outcome, lying will eventually become less and less as you use truth in words, and use deeds as your new shield.

- Humans in general have been conditioned to lie.

- It takes no religious messiah to save this planet from evil.

- Do not think that it cannot happen to your Nation?

- Let someone else fix it, just leave you alone with your television, computer, and Smartphone.

- There is only what you see and experience around you each day.

- Use the internet as a tool to dumpster dive thru the data that exists, and find out for yourself the truth of history. It will be like peering thru a prism. Separate the colors and witness the beauty of the rainbow of ideas, and truth from so many humans on this planet that wish to be free and live, and I mean live as we all were meant to be. We as humans have the ability to do whatever we wish, as long as we do not interfere with nature's laws. Of course, we have, thus our current dilemma. In order to re-balance ourselves, we will have to change our habits that directly affect the planet. That in itself will require a tremendous effort from everyone.

- There will be those of private security forces that will defend the selfless interests of the ones that now control America and the rest of planet earth. We say to them, make your choice, for what we offer you, will be greater than any promise made you.

- The government of America will benefit from the greatness of its resource, which are its people.

- The military is made up of volunteers from the total population of America, thus its existence. Without it, America would have been conquered by many other nations.

- The professional careers are far too few, and the ones that have worked so hard have been let go without good reason creating even more discord and unrest in America.

- There is an awful lot of planning that must be done in order to change the entire system of government.

- The potential of extinction of us all will come from those that make the rules for others.

- Those who are aware of the world around them will also have the same opportunity to change for the better of all humans.

- Lies and deceit have eventually lead to theaters of war within the community or even the entire Nation.

- Religious differences and ignorance have killed more people over time than all the diseases and wars that have ever plagued humankind in history!

- I find that religious ignorance plays an important role in most wars and conflicts.

- What you do from this day forward will set the stage of your future. So consider your decisions.

- There are reasons why allot of you are living good, living bad, suffering, dying, and just existing. You know how you truly feel about yourself and your life, and if given that one opportunity to truly change it, you most likely would.

- We all must get out and talk to The People in our communities. By talking to The People, we can possibly eliminate so many misunderstandings. Go talk to The People in your family, your neighbors, your neighborhood, your city, your state, your Nation, and your planet. We must strive to make this planet as one with its people. If people can accept their differences and realize that we all live in different rooms in the same house, then maybe we all can become a Human Race!

- Every American must stand with its Military, support and demand a change in government.

- It is very difficult to get rid of desire, thus the problem.

- Fear is universal in all humans, and can be used for, or against one another.

- There is no God that will save you now, only the sincere effort of each one of you working together for a common goal of freedom and liberty.

- It can be done with everyone's consent.

- What is your pleasure? It is very simple, break away from the wealthy, and let them clean themselves.

- Break away from the celebrities and let them entertain themselves for without your support to pick up after them, see them, and hear them their empires will soon crumble into dust.

- Differences make us all human beings on planet earth.

- What do stars do? They shine!

- A bored mind can CREATE!

- Americas most precious National Treasure is its people, for without it America is only a nation of land. In order for a government to be able to truly govern The People, it must believe that The People are entitled to inalienable rights, of which a few are life, liberty and a pursuit of happiness.

- *To boldly go where no human has gone before!*